A Guide for Statistics in the Behavioral Sciences

A Guide for Statistics in the Behavioral Sciences

Jeff Foster

MOMENTUM PRESS
HEALTH

MOMENTUM PRESS, LLC, NEW YORK

A Guide for Statistics in the Behavioral Sciences

First published in 2016 by
Momentum Press, LLC
222 East 46th Street, New York, NY 10017
www.momentumpress.net

ISBN-13: 978-1-60650-889-3 (paperback)
ISBN-13: 978-1-60650-890-9 (e-book)

Momentum Press Child Clinical Psychology "Nuts and Bolts" Collection

Cover and interior design by Exeter Premedia Services Private Ltd., Chennai, India

First edition: 2016

10 9 8 7 6 5 4 3 2 1

Printed in the United States of America.

Abstract

This book is a learning tool and reference guide for individuals who are confronted with statistical or research terminology commonly used in the behavioral sciences, whether it be psychology, education, communication, political science, or any of dozens of other fields that study society and individual differences. The book provides an overview of common statistical terms, techniques, and processes.

This book has two goals. The first is helping readers become better consumers of statistics so they can better understand and interpret results presented to them. The second is presenting information that can be useful for statistics and research methods courses. Unlike most standard textbooks, which are often much longer and more detailed, this book reviews standard statistical concepts and techniques at a very high level using easy-to-understand language and real world examples.

Each section includes a general review of the topic, relevant key terms, an example, and a story or illustration that highlights key points and questions. Topics fall within to general areas. The first is measurement and research basics, which covers types of scales, item writing, translations, study design, reliability, and validity. The second is statistical calculations and analyses, including descriptive statistics, distributions, t-tests, analysis of variance (ANOVA), chi-square, correlation, and regression. The introduction covers many basic statistical concepts and the concluding section presents suggestions for presenting your own statistical results.

Keywords

analyses, anthropology, behavioral sciences, correlation, education, nursing, probability, psychology, regression, research, sociology, statistics

Contents

Acknowledgments

I would like to thank Hogan Assessment Systems for giving me the opportunity to write my first statistics pocket guide. It served as the starting point for this book. It was also a great privilege and learning experience.

Introduction

"Lies, damn lies, and statistics"
Benjamin Disraeli—via Mark Twain (and others)

Most of us have heard the phrase "numbers don't lie." Yet, depending on how, why, and who is presenting them, numbers can be very misleading.

Therefore, it is important that consumers of statistical results understand what the results mean and their potential limitations. This is particularly true within behavioral sciences where we are often presented with statistics on a daily basis.

The purpose of this book is to serve as a learning tool and reference guide for individuals who are confronted with statistical or research terminology commonly used in the behavioral sciences, whether it be psychology, education, communication, political science, or any of dozens of other fields that study society and individual differences. The book provides an overview of common statistical terms, techniques, and processes. With this information, you can be better equipped to make better data-based inferences and decisions.

One of the largest problems with statistics is that they are often presented using complex formulas that most people find difficult to read. For example, the "Be on the Lookout" section of this Introduction walks through a complex-looking formula that is actually very simple—and one many people can do in their heads with small sets of numbers.

Similarly, it is easy to get lost in terms for specific kinds of analyses like *t*-tests, ANOVA, and multiple regressions (all chapters in Section 2). Most standard textbooks designate long chapters to each of these topics that are littered with formulas, statistical assumptions, variations to the analyses, and other complex issues involving that specific approach. While certainly essentially for fully understanding a specific statistical technique, only a small percentage of individuals (usually full time statisticians and professors) need this information.

Instead, the intent of this book is to cover individual topics as briefly as possible using a format that is easily digestible. Each topic is broken up into four sections:

1. A review of the topic;
2. Key terms related to the topic;
3. A real-world example; and
4. An area labeled "Be on the Lookout" that provides a story or illustration aimed at highlighting key points or questions relating to that section, many of which help illustrate how people can use statistics to mislead or confuse people.

Here is the first set of key terms to get you started.

Key Terms

- *Construct or variable*: Anything that varies and can be measured.
- *Measure, test, or assessment (n.)*: Any scale or set of items intended to assign numerical values to a construct of interest.
- *Items*: The individual items or ratings that comprise a measure, test, or assessment.
- *Scales*: Combinations of items intended to represent a specific construct or variable (e.g., job satisfaction, job performance, general mental ability).
- *Population*: The group or groups of interest in a study.
- *Sample*: Anyone or anything for which a researcher has data.
- *Sample size*: The number of participants or data points in a researcher's sample.
- *Independent variable (IV) or predictor variable*: Inputs or causes (e.g., education level, eating habits, political affiliation). In most studies, a researcher examines the impact of one or more independent variables on outcome or output variables.
- *Dependent variable (DV) or criterion or outcome variable*: Outcomes or outputs (e.g., earned income, physical health, voting behaviors).

Examples

First, here are some examples of how the first several key terms relate to one another on a single set of measurements someone might take.

Variables	Measure	Population	Items	Sample
Final performance	Number of correct answers	Stats 101 students at a university	Each item on the test	Students in three sections of Stats 101
Temperature	Degrees Celsius	Average highs for the month of July	The high temperature each day	High temperatures from every day in July for the last 30 years
Political views	A survey with 20 political questions	Adults in a specific city	Each of the 20 items on the survey	100 adults walking down the sidewalk

Next, consider a scenario where a researcher wants to investigate the potential relationships between how much time adults spend watching TV and weight loss. To determine if a relationship exists, they collect data from 200 adults who visit clinics throughout a large metropolitan area for regular physical check-ups. Here is a rundown of how several of the key terms presented earlier might relate to such a study:

- Construct or variable: The constructs or variables of interest in this case are (1) time spent watching TV and (2) weight loss.
- Measure, test, or assessment (n.): One might measure these constructs using (1) a survey asking people to track their TV time and (2) either a question asking about their history of weight loss or gain or by tracking their weight over time.
- Items: Items might include (1) asking a person how many minutes they spent watching TV each day for a three-week period and (2) asking them to weigh themselves once a week for a month.

- Scales: Time spent watching TV is pretty straightforward and likely wouldn't require the use of combining results into scales. But for physical fitness, one would ideally measure weight regularly for as long as possible to assess not just weight loss but overall patterns in weight loss or gain. You could also look at other indicators of physical fitness such as percent of body fat or body mass index (BMI).
- Population: All adults (although likely limited to a specific country or region, such as all adults in the United States).
- Sample: The adults they were able to collect data from.
- Sample size: 200 in this case.
- Independent variable (IV): Time spent watching TV is the most likely IV in this case if we assume that TV time leads to weight loss or gain. But because this study deals with associations between variables, we can't say that one variable actually causes the other (see Chapter 4).
- Dependent variable (DV): The most likely DV in this case is weight loss.

Be on the Lookout

Do you know what this is an equation for?

$$\bar{X} = \frac{\sum_{i=1}^{n} X_i}{n}$$

If you don't know, I'll give you a hint … it is probably the most common statistical formula we use and almost everyone knows how to compute it, even if you can't read the equation.

Answer

In many cases, the key to understanding research results is to cut through statistical jargon and aim for a basic understanding of the analyses a person used and what results from those analyses mean.

Even in rooms full of smart people, only a small percentage typically recognizes this formula. It is for calculating a mean (or average). In other words, this intimidating formula simply tells people to do two things: (1) add up all of their numbers and (2) divide by how many numbers they have. If you give people a handful of numbers, most people will know how to compute their average. But if you give them this formula, few will know what to do.

Here is how this formula works. First, here is the formula again:

$$\bar{X} = \frac{\sum_{i=1}^{n} X_i}{n}$$

Second, as an example, we'll use the following set of numbers:

4, 8, 3, 7, 2

Next, here is what all of the symbols in the formula stand for:

- $\bar{X}$ (with the bar above it) is the symbol for our mean, which is what we're trying to compute.
- X (without the bar above it) represents our individual numbers.
- Each individual number is designated with a subscript. For example, X_1 would be the statistical symbol "4" in our set of numbers because that is the first number listed, X_2 would be the symbol for "8" in our set because that is the second number listed. X_3 is "3," and so on. Those aren't in the actual formula, but it's important to know for the following explanation.
- i is kind of like the generic version of our subscript. When we see X_i in the formula, it tells us we're doing something with at least some of our numbers, but we have to look elsewhere in the formula to know which ones and what we're doing with them (see the following).
- n is our sample size, which is how many numbers we have (five in our case).
- $\sum$ is sigma, which in statistical formulas, means we need to add up everything that follows it.

So with that, here is how to average our numbers using the formula:

- The $\overline{X}$ just tells us what we're trying to solve for. So what is after the equal sign is what we have to do to calculate $\overline{X}$.
- After the equals sign, we have two parts to our formula, the numerator (above the line) and denominator (below the line). The numerator is the most confusing part.
- In that, we have a sigma, which tells us to add a bunch of things up. After the sigma is X_i, which tells us we are going to add up some of our numbers, but we don't know which ones yet.
- To figure that out, we first look below the sigma, where it says $i = 1$. That means that, when determining which numbers to add up, we should start with the first one in our series (i.e., start with the "4").
- We then look above the sigma to determine how far into our series to go. In this formula, there is an n above our sigma, which the symbol for our sample size. Because we have five numbers, that means we need to go five deep into our series when adding things up.
- In other words, that whole part involving the sigma simply tells us to start with the first number in our series and keep adding them until we get to the end.
- Then, we divide by n (5) to get our average, which turns out to be 4.8 in this case.

So, we can walk through complexities of the formula one by one, or we can simply add up our numbers, divide by 5, and get our answer of 4.8.

SECTION 1

Measurement and Research Basics

CHAPTER 1

Type of Scales

When most people think of measuring something, they likely think of things relating to physical size like height, distance, and square footage. However, measurement can mean different things. The most common way to measure something is to take a characteristic that varies and assign it a number (e.g., temperature, time of day, IQ, income). But, placing people or objects into groups based on individual characteristics is also a form of measurement (e.g., eye color, race and ethnicity, the size of your soda—small, medium, or large).

Different types of measures require different types of scales. And although many statistics books usually don't devote more than a page or two to outlining different types of scales, it is critically important in determining what analyses you should run and how you interpret your results.

Often times, there may be more than one way to measure the same construct. For example, although race or ethnicity has historically been viewed as a categorical variable, genetic testing can now identify what percentage of an individual's genes are from ancestors in different regions of the world, effectively redefining race or ethnicity and the type of scale we can use to measure it. In this section, we cover the most common types of scales used for data collection, terms often used to describe different scales, and examples of both using scale type correctly and incorrectly.

The most common distinctions between scale types are between categorical versus continuous data or the four slightly more elaborate scale types presented as follows (starting with "Nominal" under Key Terms). When running basic statistical analyses, knowing which of the analytical methods you should use from Section 2 often starts with knowing what types of scales you have.

For example, if you have two continuous variables, you are most likely to use a correlation to see if they are related to one another (Chapter 12). But if you have two categorical variables, you are more likely to use a

Chi-Square (Chapter 11). Other distinctions depend on factors such as the number of variables you have and how many different groups you are comparing, but variable type is always the primary starting point in determining which analyses are most appropriate.

Key Terms

- *Categorical or qualitative data*: Categorical and qualitative data essentially mean the same thing. Both refer to placing people, subjects, or other constructs of interest into discrete categories (e.g., males versus females, managers versus subordinates, fruits versus vegetables). For this reason, they are also called "discrete" variables. But the main thing to remember is that any of these terms deal with any kind of scale that simply places subjects into different groups.

- *Continuous or quantitative data*: Continuous and quantitative data also mean essentially the same thing. Both refer to measuring constructs of interest using scales that range from low to high values, such as temperature, height, and intelligence. The key to measuring something using continuous or qualitative scales is that you assign something a numerical value and higher numbers indicate a greater degree of whatever you are trying to measure. Explanations of truly continuous data usually specify that results can take any number of points because they can include decimals. For example, if you could measure finishing time in a race using an atomic clock, you would have nearly an endless number of potential outcomes. But, many measures with more limited options, such as a 0 to 100 score on a test, with only raw scores as an option, or responses to Likert scales (see the following) are also often treated as continuous scales in most common statistical analyses.

- These can be further broken down into four scale types.
  - *Nominal scale*: When talking about specific scale types, "nominal" is the term used for nearly any categorical scale. As this term suggests, nominal data involve naming or

assigning particular values into discrete categories (e.g., males versus females, experimental versus control groups, different eye colors).

○ *Ordinal scales*: These scales are used to rank order sample members on a particular construct, such as the order one finishes in a race. Because ordinal scales usually assign a numeric value to placement (e.g., first, second, third), they are typically treated as continuous scales in statistical analyses, although specific techniques may vary when dealing with ordinal data. Luckily, most statistical programs automatically make these adjustments if you specify that you are using ordinal data. And in the behavioral sciences, ordinal data aren't very common. Even with obviously ordinal scales, such as finishing place in a race, we would still typically use a different metric, such as actual finishing time or overall score, to represent scores for each subject.

○ *Interval scales*: These scales are used to assign a specific numerical value to a construct of interest, where values represent equal intervals. Examples are dates, personality measures, and temperature. Interval scales may contain the number zero, but only as an additional point of measurement (i.e., a temperature of 0°C does not mean that there is no longer a temperature). This means that they can often include negative values, such as a temperature that is below 0°C. Another difference between an ordinal scale and interval is that with ordinal, there could be a huge gap between first and second places but almost no gap between second and third. So, you can't treat those differences as the same. But with interval, a difference of 1 second is always 1 second, whether it is the difference between 10 and 11 seconds or 110 and 111 seconds. Differences between whole numbers always represent the same interval, hence the name of the scale.

○ *Ratio scales*: These are similar to interval scales, but the point at which the scale hits zero means there is an absence of what is being measured (e.g., height, weight, number correct on a test, number of days absent from a job). This also means that with true ratio scales, doubling a value always means you now have twice as much of that value. For example, if you have $2 but double that to $4, you now have twice as much. Double it again to $8 and you again have twice as much. You can't say that with interval scales like degrees in Fahrenheit—8° is not "twice as hot" as 4°.

- *Raw scores*: These are numbers assigned to any given attribute. An initial score on any measure is a raw score.
- *Percentile scores*: They provide one means for converting raw scores into a metric that can be used to compare any specific score to others in a sample. Percentile scores are derived from cumulative frequencies (see Chapter 7). For example, an individual who weighs the same or more than 3/4 of his or her preschool class is at the 75th percentile.
- *Likert scales*: These scales are often used to collect performance ratings or survey responses from individuals. They have a certain number of points (typically anywhere from 3 to 10) with lower numbers representing a small degree of or absence of something (e.g., "Strongly Disagree," "Never") and higher numbers representing a large degree or totality of something (e.g., "Strongly Agree," "Always"). Likert scales are somewhat unique because they aren't specifically interval or ratio scales. But, statistical analyses typically treat interval and ratio scales the same way, so the distinction isn't usually important in practical terms.

Examples

Table 1.1 provides an example of several variables from a call center. The types of scales for each of these variables are:

- Nominal scales: Employee #, gender;
- Ordinal scales: Rank order for conversions;

Table 1.1 Data collected from a group of call center employees

Employee #	Age	Gender	# of calls per hour	# of calls converted per week	Rank order for conversions	Supervisory performance rating
1	23	Male	17	73	3	5–Exceptional
2	32	Male	23	63	6	2–Needs improvement
3	25	Female	8	22	10	1–Unacceptable
4	27	Female	22	57	7	2–Needs improvement
5	23	Male	16	72	4	4–Strong
6	21	Male	15	53	8	3–Acceptable
7	22	Female	22	82	1	5–Exceptional
8	24	Male	27	64	5	4–Strong
9	23	Female	25	74	2	5–Exceptional
10	28	Male	17	52	9	3–Acceptable

- Interval scales: Supervisory performance ratings; and
- Ratio scales: Age, # of calls per hour, # of calls converted per week.

A few important things to note from these data include:

1. Employee number looks like a continuous scale, but it isn't. That could just as easily include letters or symbols, so it is no different than essentially renaming each employee.
2. Is it correct to say that individuals with an overall supervisory rating of 3 (Acceptable) are three times better than individuals with an overall rating of 1 (Unacceptable)? Probably not. Also, although most people would treat this as an interval scale, it is important to understand how these ratings were made and how they were described to the people making them.
3. On the ordinal scale, notice that the differences in calls converted from the top to second rated person is a difference of eight calls per week while the difference between the second and third ranked persons is only one call per week. This is an example of how you don't need to have equal intervals between numbers on ordinal scales.
4. Although the number of calls per hour seems like a fine metric for determining performance, it is insufficient if the company actually cares most about the number of calls that are converted into sales. Notice that Employee #8 makes the most calls per hour, but Employee #7 actually converts the most calls into sales.

Be on the Lookout

Figure 1.1 shows the average number of fatal accidents per 1,000 drivers for different age groups. According to these results, teenage drivers are actually safer than people in their early-20s and about equally as safe as people in their late-20s. Yet, anyone with teenagers knows that these differences are not reflected in their insurance premiums. What could be impacting these results to make it appear as though teenagers are safer than individuals in their 20s?

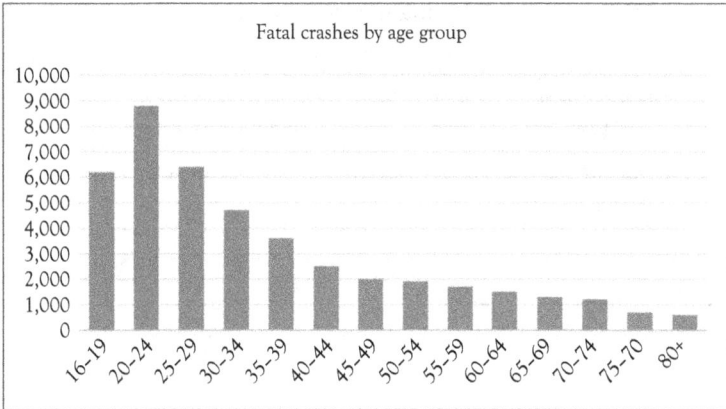

Figure 1.1 Number of drivers in fatal crashes by age

Source: Williams, A.F., and O. Carston. 1989. "Driver Age and Crash Involvement." *American Journal of Public Health* 79, no. 3, pp. 326–27.

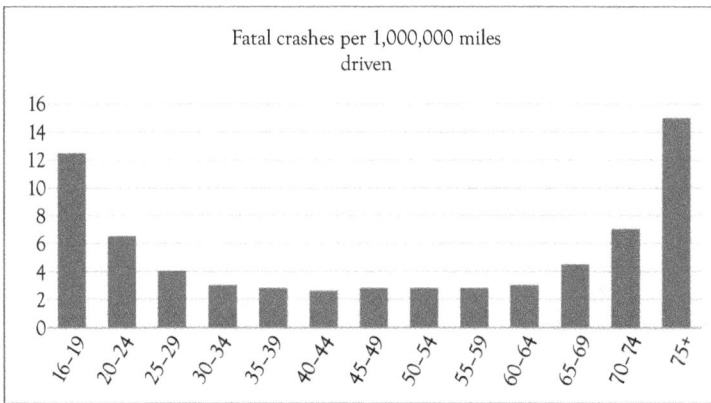

Figure 1.2 Number of fatal crashes by miles driven

Source: Williams, A.F., and O. Carston. 1989. "Driver Age and Crash Involvement." *American Journal of Public Health* 79, no. 3, pp. 326–27.

Answer

The data are correct, but they don't take into account how much teenagers drive compared to individuals of other ages. In terms of overall safety, accident per mile driven is a better indicator of driving ability than accident per person. Figure 1.2 provides those results.

This isn't an example of using the wrong overall kind of scale because both are ratio in this case, but it does illustrate the problem of using the wrong underlying metric. The first graph is fine in terms of determining who, on average, is most likely to have accidents. It does not, however, reflect actual driving safety across different age groups in terms of who you are safest with when you get into a car with someone.

CHAPTER 2

Writing Items

Another topic that usually received little attention in statistic textbooks is item writing. Nearly every piece of data we collect, especially when studying individual characteristics with human subjects, comes from items someone at some point had to write. Any kind of measure that relies on techniques such as a survey, an opinion poll, an aptitude test, or an interview depends on quality items for the results to have any meaning.

Perhaps the most surprising thing about item writing is how difficult it is to do. And in many cases, such as educational testing and personality, estimates of the number of items a person has to write to get just one good item can range anywhere from 5 to more than 20. So while often ignored, item writing is critical to nearly all research in behavioral sciences.

Key Terms

- *Response rates*: This can mean how frequently individuals respond to different survey items or how often they select different possible outcomes on an item (e.g., percentage overall who report their gender or the percentage who are male versus female).
- *Confidential*: It is usually taken to mean that results from individual respondents will not be shared with anyone, although one might still collect information about the person when collecting data. In other words, you can still ask a subject to report their name and other potentially identifying information such as gender, age, and so on, but you cannot share that information or those data with anyone not involved in conducting the study. You can still report results at the group level, such as average scores for a class on a final exam, but not at the individual level, such as how a specific individual scored.

- *Anonymity*: When a researcher does not collect any identifying information from respondents (i.e., no personal information that could later be used to determine who provided what responses), it is called anonymity. This is different from confidential data collection in that you cannot collect any identifying information at all from the subject.
- *Response bias*: Response bias is the tendency for someone to answer questions in an odd or misleading fashion. It can take many different forms. For example, some people prefer using the middle point on scales, which is a specific form of response bias called central tendency bias, while others are more comfortable using all points on the scale. Another common form is acquiescence bias, which is a general tendency to want to provide positive ratings, or say "yes" or "true" to items rather than "no" or "false." The best way to minimize response bias is by writing clear items and to make sure your instructions are as clear as possible. You can also provide sample questions and examples of different responses. This often helps subjects understand what you are asking and help make sure that different people interpret the questions the same way.
- *Reverse scored items*: These are items that measure the low end of a scale, so you literally reverse their scoring (e.g., changes responses of Strongly Agree to Strongly Disagree and vice versa) before using them to compute a total scale score. For example, if you want to determine how likely a person is to take risks at work, you might use items like "I enjoy taking risks," and "Sometimes you just have to take chances," but also include "I am very cautious when making decisions." This not only allows you to determine if respondents are accurately reading and responding to questions, but also approaches the topic from a different perspective.

Examples

One activity that nearly all of us will be involved in throughout our life is performance appraisals, the most common of which is receiving job performance ratings from one's employer or supervisor. Given the potential significance of performance ratings on one's livelihood and career, it is an area that is both difficult and important. Key considerations when writing any items, and how they pertain specifically to performance ratings, include:

1. Look at what others have done. For example, what has the organization used to measure job performance in the past? Or can you find examples of different performance ratings online or in instructional material through a class, lecture, or university? Pre-existing measures are not necessarily good ones, but they provide an idea of how others have attempted to define and measure the same characteristics in the past.

2. Identify and talk to people who represent your intended target audience. Anytime a researcher collects data, they will eventually present results to others, even if only in a written report. For job performance, you need to make sure the terminology you use makes sense to others in your company. If the intended audience is an academic one, such as published results in a peer review journal, you should be prepared to make an argument for why your items are new or better than similar items others may have used in the past.

3. Pilot test items prior to large scale data collection. No one wants to collect data and then realize he or she should have used better items. Pilot testing items with a small sample can help identify potentially confusing items or instructions and provide one with an idea of what to expect in terms of responses.

In addition, here is a list of tips relating specifically to item writing itself.

- Clarity of wording: Obviously, items need to be clear and easy for others to understand. This is where pilot testing can be a huge help. And you don't have to just give people items. You can also run focus groups where you ask subjects what they think about when they read and respond to the items.
- Strength of wording: Adjectives matter can have a dramatic effect on item responses. For example, asking someone if he

or she prefers one political party over another is not the same as asking if he or she would ever vote for the other party. You have to make sure you know exactly what you want to ask first (e.g., are you concerned about general political leanings or if someone could ever be persuaded to vote for a candidate in his or her least preferred party).

- Avoid double meanings: A person writing an item knows the intended meaning of the item, but others reading the item might not. For example, "works well with customers" could mean customers generally tend to like an employee, that the employee deals well with customer complaints, or the employee is good at getting customers to commit to a sale. Be specific with your items so their meaning is clear.

- Avoid "double barreled items": The best items are those that ask about only one thing. For example, if concerned about health-related behaviors, you could ask "Do you frequently exercise and maintain a healthy diet?" Although both questions are health-related, many people do one of these things but not the other. Instead, these should be broken out into two separate questions.

- Variance is important: Although covered more thoroughly in Chapter 7, for item writing purposes, variance means you need a variety of responses. If you ask a classroom of children if they like receiving presents and they all say yes, then you have no variance in your variable and cannot do anything with it. Both items and response formats need to be written so respondents are likely to use a variety of response options.

- Items should always match their stem: Stems are short lead in statements generally used for a large number of items (e.g., "I enjoy ..." or "I would describe myself as ..."). Not all items require a stem, but when using one, all items need to flow well and make grammatical sense according to that stem. For example, an item stem of "How often does this employee": works fine for "meet his or her goals" because you can complete a grammatically correct sentence out of those two phrases: "How often does this employee meet his or her goals?" But that stem would not work for "demonstrates exceptional job performance," because "How often does this employee demonstrates exceptional job performance?" is not grammatically correct.

- Items should always match their rating scale: Unfortunately, people mess this one up all of the time. For example, if asking behavioral items (e.g., "I watch the evening news"), the rating scale should be behavioral or frequency based (e.g., "never," "sometimes," or "always"). Behavioral items often don't work as well with agreement scales that use responses such as "Strongly Disagree" to "Strongly Agree." After all, if a person typically watches the evening news but occasionally misses it, does that mean they should disagree with this item?

- Watch out for loaded questions: Political surveys run rampant with loaded questions that can be very misleading. For example, in the United States, conservative news outlets often like to report results like "Over 80 percent of all Americans agree that they don't want the government telling them what doctor they have to go to" while liberal outlets say things like "Over 80 percent of all Americans agree that sick people should be able to receive health care." Although these results may be presented in a way that seems contradictory, where one appears in opposition to universal health care and one appears to be in support of it, the fact is that most people would agree with both of those questions. But they are written and used in a way to try to persuade people toward one side of the topic or the other.

Finally, there are some statistical methods for controlling for response bias, which is often called *rater effects* when used to describe different biases individuals have when rating the performance of others. These methods are typically only useful when a respondent rates several targets, such as a supervisor providing ratings for three or more subordinates. Another way to help with response bias is through *Frame of Reference (FOR) training*, where a researcher provides detailed instructions to raters concerning what each potential response option means, such as examples of good and bad teamwork. Finally, *Behavioral Anchored Rating Scales (BARS)* are another method of trying to reduce rater error or response bias. With BARS, specific examples of behaviors representing different ratings are provided to respondents to illustrate what different points on the rating scale represent.

Be on the Lookout

Part 1: Sample Items

What problems or potential issues can you identify in the following examples?

Rate the performance of our current President from 1 (needs improvement) to 5 (exceptional) in each of the following areas.

The current President:

1. Works well with others
   ☐ 1   ☐ 2   ☐ 3   ☐ 4   ☐ 5
2. Is loyal to his or her party and constituents
   ☐ 1   ☐ 2   ☐ 3   ☐ 4   ☐ 5
3. Is an inspiration
   ☐ 1   ☐ 2   ☐ 3   ☐ 4   ☐ 5
4. Is detailed and accurate in his or her work
   ☐ 1   ☐ 2   ☐ 3   ☐ 4   ☐ 5

How much do you agree with the following statements?

1. The President cares about me.
   ☐ Disagree   ☐ Neutral   ☐ Agree
2. I trust the President.
   ☐ Disagree   ☐ Neutral   ☐ Agree
3. The government provides for my needs.
   ☐ Disagree   ☐ Neutral   ☐ Agree
4. Makes me proud to be a citizen of my country.
   ☐ Disagree   ☐ Neutral   ☐ Agree

Part 2: New Coke

In 1985, Coca-Cola released New Coke (which wasn't called New Coke at its release but there was "NEW!" on the can so the name took hold). They had mountains of data showing that people preferred the new slightly sweater flavor over the original. They had been slowly losing market share and thought the new formula might curb their slide.

Shortly after its release, there were protests and boycotts throughout the United States, particularly in the Southeast where Coca-Cola is head-quartered and has a strong following. Although their research appeared sound because people really did generally prefer the new formula in blind taste tests, how could they have missed predicting such a strong negative response from Coke loyalists?

Answers

Part 1: There are several problems throughout these items. Some examples include:

1. The item "Works well with others" is a bit problematic because "others" can be a lot of different people such a Congress, citizens, foreign dignitaries, and so on.
2. The same could be said for "The government provides for my needs" because needs can mean different things to different people.
3. The item "Is an inspiration" does not follow the stem "The current President."
4. "Makes me proud to be a citizen of my country" isn't a complete statement.
5. The item "Is loyal to his or her party and constituents" is double loaded in that it asks about two different things (the party itself and its constituents).
6. The item "The President cares about me" isn't too bad, but the fact is, there is no way to really know what the President actually cares about. A better item might be "Seems to care about his or her constituents."

Part 2: New Coke

Although there is still debate over exactly what went wrong, part of the problem was that Coca-Cola was asking the wrong question—or at least it failed to ask all of the right questions. Although people in blind taste generally preferred the new flavor, the researchers didn't ask loyal customers what they would do if Coca-Cola changed its formula. In other words, what Coca-Cola really wanted to know was if consumers would be more likely to buy more Coke if it changed its existing formula. By failing to ask this question more directly, the company ignored the importance of customer loyalty.

As it turns out, its sales actually increased substantially when they reintroduced the original formula under "Coca-Cola Classic," leading some to conclude that New Coke was an elaborate ruse designed to stir up loyalty in its customer base and increase brand recognition, which in turn led company president Donald Keough to famously state "We're not that dumb, and we're not that smart."

CHAPTER 3

Translations

Translating any item from one language to another may seem relatively simple, but failing to follow a rigorous and accurate translation process can very easily lead to confusing and inaccurate results. It is easy to suffer from the assumption that all you need to do is find someone fluent in both languages (i.e., their original language and the new "target" language) and just have that person create a translation. But even relatively simple translations like basic demographic questions can be more complex than they seem. For example, race or ethnicity varies by country, different job titles often mean very different things in different companies, let alone across different countries, and even age can be tricky because in some Asian cultures, individuals are considered "1" when they are first born.

Consumers should always be cautious, therefore, when reviewing or interpreting any results comparing responses from individuals or cultures who speak different languages. This is especially true for opinion surveys, where even slight differences in language meaning or strength of wording can significantly influence results.

Key Terms

- *Forward translation*: When one or more individuals conduct an initial translation of items from one language to a new target language.
- *Back or backward translation*: When another person or individual then translates those new items back to the original language. This is often a useful way of identifying any problems in item content or meaning that might have resulted from the initial forward translation. If content or strength of wording is dramatically different, something got off with either the forward or backward translation (or both).

- *Application*: When one tries to translate an item into a new language as literally as possible, they have the exact same meaning. Very straightforward constructs like gender, household income, and many items on standardized tests often lend themselves well to application.
- *Adaptation*: When a translator modifies an item during the translation process, as needed, to try to ensure cultural relevance. For example, it might not make sense in some countries to ask about their president or congress but you can ask similar questions based on how they define their leadership (e.g., prime minister and parliament).
- *Assembly*: When rather than conducting direct translations, a translator writes new items intended to measure the same construct, although item wording and content might be completely different. This is often necessary for items that simply do not make sense or would be inappropriate in a different culture. For example, "I would like to drive a race car" might not be meaningful in countries where auto racing is not an available pastime, or "I like to travel to other countries" might not make sense for individuals living in countries where traveling is very restricted (or in Europe where it is much more accessible and common).

Examples

Although there are multiple processes one might use to develop new translations of an item, most effective processes share the same general characteristics. Consider three personality questions relating to extraversion, which reflects the degree to which someone seems social and outgoing: (a) "I enjoy being in crowds," (b) "I prefer going to parties over staying home," and (c) "Large gatherings make me nervous"—this one is reverse scored.

1. First, involve multiple people in the process. Although these items may seem fairly straightforward, if you ask three people to translate

them all into the same new target language, you will inevitably get three different responses. Particularly problematic can be descriptive works like "enjoy" and "nervous" that often have a number of words with very similar, yet slightly different, meanings in both their original and target language.

2. To aid in the translation process, initial item writers should avoid local idioms (e.g., "toot your own horn," or "if it feels good do it") because they are often difficult to translate into other languages. Also, unless a scale is designed to measure any of these specific topics, it is often best to avoid questions that might not go over well in some cultures, such as questions about politics, religion, topics related to valuing diversity, and so on.

3. Translators need to not only be fluent in both languages, but familiar with both cultures and be able to understand the purpose and content of the items. For example, it is often best to have someone with a background in the field of research involved in the process of translating items, such as someone with a psychological background when translating items regarding personality, attitudes, and so on. This can be particularly useful for items like "I prefer going to parties over staying home." In this case, parties can mean very different things in different cultures. A person familiar with both cultures and the overall intent of the item, which is to measure how outgoing and social a person is, can help adapt this item into something that still measures extraversion but might have a slightly altered meaning. That could be something that is more specific to the types of voluntary social gatherings available in that country (adaptation) or something with an entirely different meaning that still gets at a person's social tendencies (assembly).

4. Pilot test items with a new group once initial translations are complete. One should also follow-up with a pilot group by asking questions such as whether or not they saw any potential issues with item wording, grammar, content, and so on. Similar to writing new items, conducting focus groups with your pilot subjects is also a good opportunity to ask what they were thinking when they read and answered the items.

Even the most thorough translation process will sometimes result in new items that aren't as effective or don't measure the same exact thing as the original. For this reason, translation should always be considered an ongoing process. It is the responsibility of test publishers to regularly analyze items, such as checking for things like similar response patterns with similar samples, to make sure items work properly. Furthermore, it is the responsibility of those using items to make sure the test publisher follows some sort of process for regularly evaluating and maintaining item translations.

First and foremost, when trying to make a decision based on data collected from items translated into multiple languages, ask about and be sure you understand the translation process. If the individuals responsible for creating translations cannot provide evidence or information regarding the thoroughness of the process and how it should reduce translation errors, then you should not place as much weight on the results until you can verify their accuracy. And if you ever get a surprising or unexpected result from translated items, then there is a good chance there is something with the items themselves.

Be on the Lookout

What are some potential issues with the following personality-related items (hint, some of these lend themselves to translation errors, others have more general concerns covered in Chapter 2)?

1. I like big cities more than the country.
2. On the weekends, I am often a couch potato.
3. I rarely get upset with other people.
4. I am always cold.
5. I often think my country is moving in the wrong direction.
6. I believe religion is more important than politics.
7. I enjoy traveling to other countries.
8. I take pride in being a good follower.

Answer

Here is a brief description of at least one potential problem with each of the items provided as examples:

1. I like big cities more than the country—Individual perceptions of what is a big city and what is the country can differ by culture.
2. On the weekends, I am often a couch potato—Not everyone knows what the phrase "couch potato" means.
3. I rarely get upset with other people—The word "upset" can easily be translated in a way that varies in terms of item strength (e.g., simply unhappy versus angry).
4. I am always cold—The problem here is a potential double meaning, where "cold" could refer to physical coldness or coldness toward others.
5. I often think my country is moving in the wrong direction—This item might not be politically appropriate in some countries.
6. I believe religion is more important than politics—This item asks about religion and politics, both of which might not be appropriate in some countries.
7. I enjoy traveling to other countries—Foreign travel is both easier and more common in some countries than others.
8. I take pride in being a good follower—The term "follower" might be translated inappropriately (e.g., "stalker"). In this case, a good back translation should reveal any major problems.

CHAPTER 4

Study Design

Study design or research method is often a topic covered as its own class in many university programs. However, it overlaps to such a large degree with statistics that it is impossible to cover one and not the other. While statistics more directly involves what we do with data once we've collected them (and yes, the term "data" is traditionally considered plural), our results are entirely dependent on the effectiveness and appropriateness of our research methods.

For example, one of the most frequently used invalid claims is that a product is scientifically proven to do something. As we'll cover in subsequent chapters, statistics is all about probabilities. Even very odd and unusual results can happen by random chance a very small percentage of the time. So when a commercial claims that research has scientifically proven that a new drug helps you lose weight, or a cream can remove wrinkles, or a supplement can ward off colds—these claims are often medically related—then the commercial's creators either don't understand how statistics work or are deliberately trying to mislead consumers. That is why it is important to understand at least the very basics of study design so that, if interested in a product that claims to have research support, you can evaluate that research with a more critical eye.

This chapter provides a brief overview of the most critical concepts and practices regarding research methods and study design.

Key Terms

- *Observational study*: Studies that collect data from individuals in ways that are not supposed to affect them (e.g., surveys, on-site observations).
- *Experiments*: Studies that impose one or more treatments or conditions on study participants.

- *Experimental or treatment group*: The group(s) that receives certain treatments (e.g., a new drug, specific instructions on how to perform a task).
- *Control group*: The group that does not receive any treatments, which then serves as a comparison or base rate group.
- *Causation*: The assumption that one variable, such as whether or not someone takes a weight loss pill, actually influences scores on another variable, such as weight loss. We cannot assume causation from observational studies, only experiments where someone has deliberately placed subjects into treatment and control groups. In other words, if someone finds that people really do lose more weight after taking a weight loss pill, it could just be that people who have elected to spend money on the pill, especially if it is expensive, are more likely to stick to a new regiment that helps them lose weight because they committed. Only if a researcher selects some people to take the pill and others to not take it can he or she reasonably conclude that the pill probably helped people lose weight. But many other aspects of study design are also critical for supporting this conclusion.
- *Sample characteristics*: The characteristics of the sample used to collect data can have a dramatic impact on a study's results. Some potential problems with sample characteristics are obvious (e.g., one wouldn't want to conduct an employee opinion survey for a company but only collect data from one department while leaving others out entirely).
- *Sampling error*: Sampling error is the bane of any researcher, especially those who collect data using human subjects. In general, it means results will vary depending on the subjects available to a researcher simply because no sample can perfectly represent an entire population of interest. For example, one reviews exam data from multiple sections of the same intro to statistics class, results will likely for no other reason than different students are in different sections. Some will inevitably include students that are more academically inclined than others. One primary goal of many of the

statistical tests outlined in the second section of this book
are to identify when statistical results (e.g., differences in
final grades between day-time sections of a class and evening
sections) are simply due to sampling error versus other more
important factors (e.g., quality of the instructors).

- *Sample bias*: When statistical results are impacted by characteristics of a sample that do not reflect sampling error but,
  instead, something that is unique about your sample compared to your population of interest. For example, trying
  to examine the impact of new student orientation training
  on incoming college freshmen might not generalize to all
  freshmen if a study just includes data from recent high school
  graduates (in which case, results might not mean the same
  thing for nontraditional students).
- *Confounding variables*: These are usually unknown variables
  that impact the relationship between the variables a researcher
  is interested in studying. Confounding variables are responsible for a large percentage of the problems we typically see
  when people present misleading statistical results. Examples of
  the impact of confounding variables are presented throughout
  this book.
- *Random sampling*: Randomly selecting study participants out
  of a total possible subject pool and placing them into treatment and control groups. The intent of random sampling is
  to help control for sample bias and confounding variables
  that can affect a study's results by spreading out people with
  different characteristics across all of your study's groups. For
  example, it is simply easier for some people to lose weight
  than others. Randomly placing people into groups, especially
  if you have a large enough sample, helps increase your chances
  of having a fairly equal number of people in each group who
  both lose weight easily and who struggle to lose weight.
- *Stratified sampling*: Selecting a certain number of participants
  with specific characteristics from a total possible subject pool.
  For example, if a researcher wants to study college freshmen,
  he or she might specifically sample a certain percentage of

participants from different major areas to make sure all are represented.

- *Convenience sample*: Convenience samples can be gathered several different ways, but as the term implies, all of them pertain to collecting data from whomever a researcher easily has access to. Collecting data from students, employees, friends, and, more recently, crowd sourcing websites are all typically considered convenience samples.

- *Representation*: How well a sample reflects the intended population of interest in terms of important individual characteristics.

- *Attrition*: When subjects drop out during the course of a study. Attrition not only results in smaller sample sizes, but often raises issues over whether or not those who drop out are different in some important way from those who do not drop out, which can result in a biased sample.

- *Generalizability*: How well results from one study or sample can be expected to apply to other samples. In other words, can one expect that results would be similar for other samples?

Examples

To illustrate the key terms in this chapter, we'll build on the sample outlined in the introduction concerning a study between how much time adults spend watching TV and their physical fitness level. Here are additional considerations in terms of study design for that scenario.

- General design: This would be an observational study, not an experiment.
- Groups: The researcher here is not able to randomly place people into groups, so there is not experimental or control group. That would require getting people to sign up for either watching predetermined amounts of TV over the study period or, for a control group, likely not watching any TV. Instead, the researcher is only able to collect data from people who visit clinics in this particular area.

- Causation: For this reason, even if watching less TV is associated with more weight loss, one cannot as confidently conclude that it is a casual relationship. Although it's fairly reasonable to conclude that weight gain or loss does not directly impact how much time someone then spends watching TV (i.e., people don't likely watch more TV *because* they are gaining weight), it could be that a third variable, such as a person's energy level, is actually responsible for changes in both TV watching and weight gain.

- Sample characteristics: They should investigate as many other potentially relevant characteristics as possible, such as basic demographics like gender, race or ethnicity, and age, as well as anything relating to previous health experiences, weight loss and gain, and variables associated with TV watching such as time spent on other activities.

- Sampling error: Two hundred is a pretty good sample size for many types of analyses, but it is still possible it isn't large enough to reflect the general adult population in this case. Perhaps people who watch less TV are generally healthy, but there could be an unusually large percentage of less healthy people who watch no TV in this sample that could throw of the study's results. See the section on correlation (in Chapter 12) and discussion of "outliers" for more information on how a few people could throw off this study's results.

- Sample bias: The largest concern over sampling error here is that the entire sample is only people who attended their doctor for a regular checkup, so results might not be the same for people who do not receive regular checkups. For example, it is possible that most people who regularly visit their doctor are healthier than the general public, so the relationship between health and TV time might not be as strong for this small percentage of the entire population, which in this case is all adults.

- Confounding variables: There are all kinds of potential confounding variables with this study. Two examples include: (1) what they watch—if some people in the sample only watch workout videos, then their health might increase as they watch more TV, or (2) type of doctor—if the only doctors included in the study regularly treated athletic injuries, then their patients could be a relatively healthy group that is simply watching more TV than usual because they are recovering from injuries.

- Sampling strategy: This is a convenience sample because the researcher can only collect data from people who happen to show up at one of the clinics and are willing to participate in the study.

- Representation: Based on other variables collected, such as basic demographics, the researcher would ideally be able to match the clinic sample as closely as possible to the adult population of the city, if not a larger geographic region. The closer the match on relevant variables that could impact the study's results, the more likely the results will represent the general population of interest.

- Attrition: If the researcher collects all of his or her data at one point in time, then attrition isn't a problem. To do that, they could just ask participants to tell them how much weight they have lost or gained over a period of time, such as the last three months. But it would likely be more ideal to measure weight repeatedly over a period of time in the future, which would likely be impossible to get from every single participant. To account for attrition, therefore, you need to not only start with more people than you need, but you need to compare those who stay in the study to those who leave at some point. For example, it could throw off the study's results if people who gain weight are more likely to drop out. In that case, it might be necessary to devote more time and effort to setting up some kind of experimental study.

- Generalizability: The key to being able to generalize results to a larger population are matching on relevant sample characteristics, accounting for confounding variables, and controlling for sample bias. The fact is, we rarely know if our results will generalize well to larger populations. But trying to minimize the potential impact of these three factors helps us be more confident.

Although this list is not all inclusive, here are several things to ask when reviewing research results presented by others.

1. What are the primary research questions?
2. What is the ideal sample to address these questions?
3. Did the sample used for data collection reflect this ideal sample as closely as possible?
4. What are the ideal measures to address the research questions?
5. Did the measures used to collect data reflect these ideal measures as closely as possible?
6. What potential confounding variables did the researcher(s) examine?
7. What potential confounding variables did the researcher(s) unaccounted for?
8. Did they use appropriate data analyses?
9. Did the report results clearly and accurately?
10. What steps did they take to ensure accuracy in data collection and analyses?
11. Who is the primary intended audience?
12. Did they report results in a manner that was effective for this audience?

Be on the Lookout

Most of us have seen the picture of Harry Truman holding up the Chicago Tribune headline proclaiming "Dewey Defeats Truman," which was clearly was not the right outcome. Unfortunately, misleading political polls existed long before the 1948 presidential election and continue to thrive today. One earlier slightly less famous example occurred shortly before the 1936 presidential election between Alf Landon and Franklin Roosevelt. A popular weekly magazine, the *Literary Digest*, included a survey that readers could mail back on a post card. Of their 10 million or so readers at the time, over 2 million responded, a truly astronomical number for any poll in any day and age. Based on these results, they concluded Landon would win by a landslide. What might have been wrong with this survey?

Answer

The *Literary Digest* poll certainly had no issues with sample error because of including results from over 2 million respondents. But sample bias was a huge problem, in large part because the poll occurred in 1936, which was well into the Great Depression. In general, the sample was over-representative of people with enough discretionary income to afford to not only purchase the *Literary Digest*, but also pay the necessary postage to mail a survey card back to the magazine. As a result, it lacked a high percentage of what turned out to be lower income Roosevelt voters.

As in all cases, sample bias in this instance can also be described as resulting in a sample that was not representative on the intended population, which was all likely U.S. voters. And how do we describe this bias or lack of representativeness? The answer is confounding variables. In this case, the primary confound was likely income, or discretionary spending. But, if readers of the *Literary Digest* generally leaned toward the Republican Party, that would have also been a confounding variable and source of sample bias.

CHAPTER 5

Reliability

In general, *reliability* refers to how consistent scores are across multiple ratings or rating sources. In other words, if a researcher tries to measure the same thing multiple times or measure it using multiple methods, how similar are his or her results? There are several types of reliability that are calculated in different ways, but in general, most result in scores that range from 0.00 (representing no reliability—or no consistency or agreement) to 1.00 (representing perfect reliability).

We generally expect measures to be very reliable. The length of time in the day, the distance between towns, and the height of a mountain generally don't change much over time. So, we would reasonably expect our measurements of these characteristics from one day to another to be nearly identical. Weather, on the other hand, often isn't very reliable. In most areas, it not only changes from day-to-day, but can change from minute-to-minute.

Individual characteristics act the same way. Some, such as the height and weight, may change gradually over time, but they are generally consistent from one day to another. In contrast, other characteristics such as energy level, mood, how social we feel, and how we feel about our coworkers are all likely to show more fluctuation, sometimes changing from one minute to the next. For most measures, reliability scores greater than 0.90 are usually considered exceptional, whereas scores that range anywhere from 0.60 to 0.70 or higher are often considered adequate. Although it depends on the purpose of the measure and the type of reliability one computes, a researcher can generally expect to raise eyebrows when any reliability coefficient falls below 0.60 or 0.50.

Key Terms

- *True score*: A hypothetical value of exactly what a score would be if it were measured perfectly.

- *Observed score*: The result a researcher actually gets when measuring something. An observed score comprises both a true score and error.
- *Error*: Anything that impacts a measure to cause the observed score to deviate from a true score. As error increases, reliability decreases. Error can result from a wide range of issues, such as problems with the measure itself (e.g., a short and inaccurate IQ test), unforeseen variables that impact the measure (e.g., how much sleep the person got the night before taking an IQ test), or an actual error (e.g., failing to properly record a person's results on an IQ test).
- *Standard error of measurement*: A calculation that determines how accurate an observed score is likely to be. In other words, it tells us how close our observed score is likely to be to the underlying true score we are interested in.
- *Confidence interval*: A range in which a true score is likely to fall. For example, if a person's score on a comprehensive and highly reliable IQ test is 100, one could use the standard error of measurement associated with the test to calculate a 95 percent confidence interval (e.g., there is a 95 percent chance that their "true" IQ is between 97 and 103). However, with a less reliable test, the confidence interval may be much larger (e.g., could be as large as 80 to 120 if reliability is low). You can actually apply confidence intervals to nearly any statistical outcome. And although the exact interpretation of confidence intervals is often confusing, one can loosely conclude that confidence intervals give us a range in which our true score or population estimate is likely to fall.

Examples

- *Split form reliability*: A reliability estimate derived from splitting a test in half and correlating scores on both halves with one another. To compute split form reliability, you correlate scores on the first half of your test with scores on the second half, and then you have to use *Kuder-Richardson Formula* (KR-20) to estimate reliability for the full set of items.

- *KR-20*: A short formula for estimating what coefficient alpha would be if items were added to or removed from a scale. Generally, more items increases reliability, regardless of what type of reliability you compute. So for example, if you compute reliability from five items, you can use KR-20 to determine what reliability would likely be if you had 10 items, 20 items, or any other larger set.

- *Coefficient (or Cronbach's) alpha*: A measure of internal consistency, or to what degree a set of items generally measure the same construct of interest. In other words, if you write a bunch of items to measure teamwork, alpha would tell you the degree to which those items generally get at the same underlying construct: teamwork. Another way to think of it is that it tells us how much items have in common. This is typically the most common form of reliability reported in the behavioral sciences, but it also has limitations (see more in the following text).

- *Test-Retest reliability*: The correlation between test scores measured at two different points in time. An example would be correlating scores from an IQ test given in January to scores on the same test given to the same people in February. This is typically the most popular alternative to coefficient alpha in the behavioral sciences.

- *Parallel forms reliability*: The correlation between two sets of items designed to be as identical to one another as possible. In other words, it is the correlation between scores on two sets of items written to measure the same construct with the same degree of difficulty.

Be on the Lookout

When someone asks what the reliability of a measure is, they are often asking about coefficient alpha. Coefficient alpha is commonly referred to as a measure of internal consistency, or the degree to which items measure the same thing.

Consider an example where researchers want to develop a measure of teamwork. They write the following five items and ask supervisors to rate 100 different employees on each item (using a 5-point Likert Scale where 1 indicates "Strongly Disagree" and 5 indicates "Strongly Agree").

This employee:

1. Is friendly and cooperative.
2. Helps other when needed.
3. Is a good team member.
4. Works well in a team.
5. Gets along well with everyone.

The resulting coefficient alpha is 0.68. Not bad, but not as high as they hoped. Follow-up analyzes using a statistical program indicate that alpha would be a much higher 0.92 with only Items 3 and 4. Even though the alpha would be higher, would this result in a better overall measure of teamwork?

Answer

Not necessarily. The problem is that the alpha is so high for the two items ("Is a good team player" and "Works well in a team") because they essentially measure the exact same thing. Granted, both are important indicators of teamwork, but additional items such as "Is friendly and cooperative" get at different aspects of teamwork that could also be important for the job. So, if the intent is to just measure how well someone works on a specific team, the simpler two-item measure might work fine. But, if the concept of "teamwork" is intended to measure how well a person works with others in a company outside of his or her team, additional items might be important even if they lower alpha to some degree.

This also shows how someone can inflate alpha by writing items that ask the same thing in slightly different ways. That doesn't mean, however, that they have a better scale in the end because it might not be as comprehensive or useful. And in this example, test-retest reliability might be just as high or higher for all five items compared to only using Items 3 and 4. So, although alpha certainly provides useful information, an over-reliance on just internal consistency ignores other forms of reliability that are often just as, if not more, important.

CHAPTER 6

Validity

Researchers have tried to come up with a consistent and comprehensive definition of validity for decades. No one has. Part of the reason is that there are dozens of different types of validity. So, when different people try to outline or argue about different definitions, they are often simply talking about different kinds of validity. However, in the most general sense, *validity* is usually meant as an indication of whether or not, or to what degree, a measure does what we want it to do. The trick is defining ahead of time exactly what you want the measure to do—that is, what you mean by validity or what type of validity you are referring to. In this chapter, we outline several of the most common forms of validity used in the behavioral sciences.

Reliability and validity are often discussed together because both are critical for drawing accurate conclusions from research results. And one common *mantra* is that you can have reliability without validity but it is not possible to have validity without reliability. In other words, if any measure is wildly inconsistent in inaccurate (low reliability), then it probably isn't going to do what you want it to do (low validity). However, a measure can have high reliability but still have little to no validity. For example, you could use a tape measure to assess the distance between a person's front door and the street. If used correctly, you should get almost the exact same measurement over and over again, which would make it reliable. But it isn't going to be a valid measure of anything other than the distance from their front door to the street. If you try to use that information as an indicator of anything else about their property, such as what street it is on, the color of the house, or how many people live there, what you'll be left with is a highly reliable measure that has almost no validity in terms of how you are trying to use it.

Key Terms

- *Validation*: It is the process that one uses to try to estimate or establish validity.
- *Utility*: Similar to validity, utility is a fairly generic term for indicating the overall value of using a measure for a specific purpose. For example, one could calculate the expected value of using a new hiring process to screen employees at a company. If this process effectively identifies job applicants who are more likely to be good employees, you could then use a form of utility analysis to compare the estimated value of using the process to the cost of the process, which would indicate its overall utility. However, if the process isn't good at identifying likely high performers, meaning that it isn't very valid, then it won't provide much utility to the company.

Examples

- *Face validity*: Whether or not a measure looks as if it measures what it is supposed to. So to continue with the hiring process example, face validity would be based on whether or not the different steps in the hiring process appear to measure things that are important for the job. If there was an interview component, face validity would depend on whether or not the questions appear to be job related, such as "Tell me about your previous experience working directly with customers," or not job related, such as "If you could be any kind of tree, what kind of tree would you be?"
- *Content validity*: Similar to face validity, but often more heavily driven by expert opinion. In terms of job interview questions, content validity depends on the degree to which individuals who know the job well (e.g., supervisors, high-performing current employees, customers) believe the interview questions cover a comprehensive range of job relevant information. So while a question about experience working with customers may appear to have strong face validity

to most applicants, it may lack content validity if those who know the job well realize that the person in the position rarely actually works directly with customers.

- *Criterion-related validity*: The extent to which a score on one measure predicts a score on some criterion or outcome measure. In terms of hiring, this is the degree to which different steps in a selection process actually predict future job performance ratings. Researchers often determine criterion-related validity by correlating scores (see Chapter 13) from something like an interview or assessment center to actual job performance ratings. There are two primary approaches to establishing criterion-related validity:

  o *Predictive validity*: A criterion-related validity study where you collect scores on a predictor, such as an interview, and compare them to job performance ratings gathered from the same people after they have been employed for a while, usually at least 6 to 12 months. Although this seems fairly straightforward, true predictive validity studies are rare because they can cost a lot of money and, by definition, take a lot of time. Few companies are willing to spend money on a selection system that they don't actually use for hiring decisions for a year or two so they can eventually see how everyone who went through the system scored and then go back and look at their job performance later.

  o *Concurrent validity*: Similar to predictive validity, but you collect scores on the predictor measure from existing employees rather than applicants. This makes it much faster and less expensive but also has limitations. First, it's rare with interviews because most people don't want to go through an artificial interview process for a job they already have. It is more used more frequently, however, with other common selection tools such as ability tests, personality tests, and other questionnaire or survey-based selection instruments. With concurrent validity, you can collect predictor scores and performance ratings at the same time, which makes the process much faster. However, you may also run into issues of sample bias. Usually, your current employees look like some, but not all, of your job applicants. After all, they represent only a sample of all applicants who you actually hired. And as companies grow and evolve, their applicant pools can also change.

- *Internal validity*: This refers to the accuracy of conclusions that can be drawn from a study, particularly in relation to determining causation from experiments. For example, to try to establish internal validity for a study determining if a diet pill helps people lose weight, researchers would need to set up the study specifically to avoid several of the potential research problems outlined in Chapter 4, such as sampling error, sample bias, and the potential for confound variables.

- *External validity*: The degree to which results from one study should generalize (again, see Chapter 4) to similar samples. So even if the diet pill seems effective based on the results of a study, external validity concerns the degree to which it should work for other people. This is based largely on sample characteristics such as the sample size and how representative it is of the intended population (i.e., anyone who might be a future customer).

Because there are so many types of validity and because related terms such as "valid" and "validate" are so common, it is easy to see why validity is often misused in the realm of research and statistics. Therefore, when hearing someone refer to validity, it is important to make sure you know what type of validity they are referring to and what evidence they have to support any validity claims they make.

Be on the Lookout

Although it's hard to find numbers relating to how frequently it is administered, the Oxford Capacity Analysis (OCA) is generally considered one of the most widely used personality tests in the world. Yet, there is very little published evidence regarding its validity. This is because the Church of Scientology uses the OCA as a common part of its recruiting efforts. Many professors and researchers who study personality and regularly publish evidence on other instruments have criticized the OCA as not being a genuine personality test, and there remains little evidence available to refute this claim. Yet, those who use it as part of recruiting efforts still claim it is valid, or at the very least discard claims to the contrary. Is it possible that individuals on both sides of this debate are correct?

Answer

One could argue that both sides on this debate are correct. When professors and researchers talk about the validity of a personality test, they are often referring to content validity, predictive validity, or other forms not discussed here such as convergent and discriminant validity (which basically mean that a scale correlates with other scales that measure similar constructs but not with other scales intended to measure different constructs). Without published evidence concerning these types of validity, it is easy to claim that the OCA is likely not very valid in these regards.

But, if we think about validity more general terms, such as whether or not a scale or assessment does what we want it to do, then the OCA is likely valid. Because the members of the Church of Scientology use it as part of their recruiting efforts, the intended purpose is to provide information that assists with these efforts. In other words, it is unlikely they would continue to use it if it didn't help with recruiting. That is why it's important to understand different types of validity and know what type someone is referring to when they claim a measure is or is not valid.

SECTION 2

Statistical Analyses

CHAPTER 7

Describing Data

The first step after collecting data is usually to start running a series of basic analyses that fall under the large umbrella of descriptive statistics. As the term suggests, *descriptive statistics* generally describe different aspects of data such as the number of people in different groups on categorical variables or average scores and score ranges on continuous variables. Descriptive statistics also help us organize, present, and describe our data to others.

Descriptive statistics usually pertain to only one variable at a time. Most analyses that deal with more than one variable are called inferential statistics because we use them to infer something about relationships between variables in our populations of interest. Those are the types of analyses covered in Chapters 9 through 13 of this book. But before running inferential statistics, most researchers start with descriptive statistics to help them better understand their data, look for errors, and describe their data to others.

You could collect any number of variables from a class (e.g., class size, attendance, scores on assignments and tests, average time spent studying) and have an entire spreadsheet full of information about that one section of that one class. And often, more data are better. But, even a fairly small dataset containing information on a dozen or so variables from 30 students can quickly turn into what looks like a sea of numbers that are too much to process all at once. Descriptive statistics help us boil down large datasets into a handful of easily digestible components. They can also be useful for seeing how data change over time, such as tracking scores in a class throughout the semester or weight loss during the course of a diet.

Key Terms

- *Frequency*: The number of scores falling at a particular value. For categorical variables, this is usually the number of people in each group. For a student sample, this could be the number of freshmen, sophomores, juniors, and seniors in your sample. For continuous variables with lots of possible scores, you usually put scores into groups and identify how many people are in each group. For example, if looking at age, you could place subjects into groups such as 0 to 9 years old, 10 to 19 years old, 20 to 29 years old, and so on.

- *Relative frequency*: The percentage of scores falling at a particular point or within a group. For example, among college students, it could be what percentage are freshmen. Or it could be the number of people receiving an A (i.e., final score ranging from 90–100) in a statistics class.

- *Cumulative frequency*: The percentage of scores falling at or below a particular point. Cumulative frequencies don't work for categorical variables, but they can be very useful for ascribing meaning to continuous variables. For example, cumulative frequencies are often used to interpret the height and weight of children as they grow. To simply say that a 2-year-old weighs 30 pounds isn't very meaningful if you don't know how much most 2-year-olds weigh. But to say that 30 pounds is at the 75th percentile for all 2-year-olds is more meaningful because it tells you that this particular 2-year-old weighs more than about 75 percent of all 2-year-olds but less than the remaining 25 percent. As scores on the variable increase, the cumulative frequency also increases (e.g., 31 pounds is around the 82nd percentile).

- *Measures of central tendency*: Measures used to indicate how data from continuous variables cluster around some value. Again, they don't work for categorical variables. The three most common measures of central tendency are:
  - *Mean*: The mathematical average. To calculate the mean, add scores on a particular variable and divide by the number of scores you have.
  - *Median*: When one lines up scores in order from lowest to highest, the median is the score that falls in the middle. If there are two scores in the middle (i.e., there is an even

number of scores), then most people average those two middle scores to get the median.

  o *Mode*: The score that shows up the most. There doesn't have to be a mode if everyone has his or her own unique score (e.g., finishing times in a race and no two people finish at the exact same time). Or, there can also be more than one mode.

- *Bimodal*: A dataset with two modes, or at least data with two different scores that show up a significant amount of the time. Height of all adults in an area is a good example because there are separate modes for males and females. There might be a few more males or females at those respective levels, but most would still describe this as a bimodal dataset where you have one most common height for males and one more common height for females.

- *Median split*: When one divides a set of scores into two groups at the median (i.e., those above the median versus those below the median).

- *Mean split*: When one divides a set of scores into two groups at the mean (i.e., those above the mathematical average versus those below the mathematical average).

- *Range*: The difference between the highest and lowest scores on a variable (i.e., highest minus lowest).

- *Interquartile range*: The difference between scores at the 75th and 25th percentiles.

- *Variance*: An indication of how spread out, or how varied, results are. To calculate it is a little lengthy, but involves (1) subtracting the mean from each individual value, (2) squaring that result for each individual value, (3) adding up all those squared values, and (4) dividing by the total number of subjects. The important thing to know is that when scores are more spread out, variance will be higher.

- *Standard deviation*: The square root of variance. It is another indication of how much scores vary from one another and serves as the foundation for a number of more complex statistical results covered in later chapters. But in general, it is similar to an average distance whose scores fall from the mean. It's not exactly an average of that distance, but it is close. So if you had a dataset with an average score of 50 and a standard deviation of 10, then on average, your scores tend to fall around 10 points away from the mean. If your standard deviation is 5, then scores tend to fall much closer, on average, to your mean score of 50.

- *Standard error of the mean*: Similar to standard error of measurement (Chapter 5) but, as the name suggests, applied to the mean or average score from an entire sample rather than each individual score. In other words, it helps determine how likely it is that your sample mean is close to your actual population mean. You can also use standard error of the mean to create confidence intervals. And like any other form of standard error, it is based primarily on sample size so that we can be more confident in a mean score if we have more people in our sample.

- *Outlier*: Any extreme score. For example, if the average score in a math examination is 80 out of 100, an individual receiving a 20 out of 100 is likely an outlier. Outliers are often identified as any score falling more than two or three standard deviations either above or below the mean.

Examples

To illustrate these concepts, Table 7.1 presents an example of scores of children from a pre-K class. As with our employee sample in Chapter 1, the student number is a nominal variable and doesn't hold any numerical meaning. Instead, our primary variable of interest is weight in pounds.

Measures of central tendency:

- *Mean* = 37.00 (24 + 26 + 35 + 38 + 38 + 38 + 39 + 39 + 40 + 42 + 42 + 43)/12 = 444/12
- *Median* = 38.5 (average of the middle two numbers, which are 38 and 39)
- *Mode* = 38 (it's the only score that shows up three times)

Table 7.1 *Weight of children in a pre-K class*

Student number	Weight in pounds	Median	Mode	Mean split	Median split	Interquartile range	Difference from the mean
1	24	24	24	Group 1	Group 1	24	-13
2	26	26	26	Group 1	Group 1	26	-11
3	35	35	35	Group 1	Group 1	35	-2
4	38	38	38	Group 2	Group 1	38	1
5	38	38	38	Group 2	Group 1	38	1
6	38	38	38	Group 2	Group 1	38	1
7	39	39	39	Group 2	Group 2	39	2
8	39	39	39	Group 2	Group 2	39	2
9	40	40	40	Group 2	Group 2	40	3
10	42	42	42	Group 2	Group 2	42	5
11	42	42	42	Group 2	Group 2	42	5
12	43	43	43	Group 2	Group 2	43	6

Note: Scores making up the median, mode, and interquartile range are highlighted in grey.

How spread out scores are:

- *Range* = 19 (43 – 24)
- *Interquartile range* = 2 (40 – 38)
- *Variance* = 33.3 (169 + 121 + 4 + 1 + 1 + 1 + 4 + 4 + 9 + 25 + 25 + 37)/12 = 400/12
- *Standard deviation* = 5.77 (Square root of 33.3)

This is a good example of when interquartile can be useful. Because of some extreme scores on the low end (24 and 26 pounds), the range is much larger than it would be without those two scores. Interquartile ranges provide us with an estimate of how bunched up scores are in the middle. In this case, it shows that the middle 50 percent of the scores are all very similar to one another (all within 2 pounds of one another).

It's also important to note there is a difference in how you calculate variance and standard deviation for your sample versus how you calculate them if you are using them to estimate variance and standard deviation in the population. When using them to estimate variance and standard deviation in the population, the results from your sample tend to be lower than what you would find in your population, especially for small samples. So, rather than dividing by N to get variance, you divide by $(N - 1)$. With a small sample, this can make a pretty big difference, such as dividing by 9 rather than 10, but with a large sample, it is only a very small correction, such as dividing by 999 rather than 1,000.

So in the previous example, if you wanted to use data from your sample to estimate the variance in weights for all pre-k children, you would divide 400 by 11 rather than 12, resulting in a new variance estimate of 36.36 and new standard deviation estimate of 6.03.

Table 7.2 is a frequency table for these same data.

Rather than listing each score separately, we now list each score that shows up in our data and in the next column, the number of people who receive that score. Note that cumulative frequency for any one score is the sum of the relative frequency plus the relative frequency for every score that falls below that score. For example, the 50 percent cumulative frequency for a raw score weight of 38 pounds is the relative frequency for that score (25 percent, which means 1/4th of all of our subjects'

Table 7.2 Same previous example reported as frequencies

Weight in pounds	Number of students (frequency)	Relative frequency (%)	Cumulative frequency (%)
24	1	8.33	8.33
26	1	8.33	16.67
35	1	8.33	25.00
38	3	25.00	50.00
39	2	16.67	66.67
40	1	8.33	75.00
42	2	16.67	91.67
43	1	8.33	100

Table 7.3 Household incomes in the United States—2009

Income level	Relative frequency (%)	Cumulative frequency (%)
Under $15K	13.0	13.0
$15–25K	11.9	24.9
$25–35K	11.1	36.1
$35–50K	14.1	50.2
$50–75K	18.1	68.3
$75–100K	11.5	79.8
$100–150K	11.9	91.8
$150–200K	4.4	96.2
$200K and up	3.8	100

Source: The United States Census Bureau at: www.census.gov/compendia/statab/cats/income_expenditures_poverty_wealth/household_income.html

weight 38 pounds) and the relative frequencies below that for 35, 26, and 24 pounds (8.33% + 8.33% + 8.33%).

Table 7.3 displays frequencies for a continuous variable based on data from hundreds of thousands of cases. And because of the large range of possible outcomes, the data have been broken up into groups based off ranges of data.

Also, outliers can dramatically impact measures of central tendency. For example, consider a class of 10 students who have a mean score of 80 out of 100 in an examination. If you replace just one person with a score of 90 and substitute in another student with a score of 10, that mean score will drop to 72 simply because of that one change. In contrast, the median is likely to only change by a couple of points, if at all.

Be on the Lookout

Part 1: *Average Income*

Results in Table 7.2 also help illustrate an important point about measures of central tendency. One issue that commonly leads to confusion concerns what specific measure of central tendency one uses to report the "average" score for a variable. Even though the mean is technically the average according to most common definitions, people will sometimes call the median the average. So, when someone reports an average score, it never hurts to ask how they came up with that average.

For example, consider the median and mean scores from the data used to create Table 7.2:

Reported Median = $49,777

Reported Mean = $67,976

When might one want to report the mean as the average? When would one want to report the median instead?

Part 2: *Traffic Accidents*

Common estimates are that more than half of all traffic accidents take place within 5 miles of a person's home. And over 3/4 occur within 15 miles. Why might this be? Does it mean that people are less likely to drive safely when closer to home?

Answers

Part 1: Average Income

Clearly, the answer here is that people tend to report the median when they want to discuss a lower number and the mean when they want to discuss a higher number. The problem is that they don't often explain which number they are using or what the differences are. This comes into play a lot in political discussions when individuals want to make certain areas or regions look poor or wealthy, and can be even more problematic with smaller areas. When reporting the average income of towns or small communities within cities, only a handful of high income earners can dramatically drive up the mean income while having no impact on median. This can result in large differences between the two different kinds of "average."

Part 2: Traffic Accidents

It is likely true that most of our accidents happen close to home, but it doesn't necessarily mean we drive more carelessly the closer we get to our own driveway or parking spot. Granted, drivers may tend to become careless and less watchful in areas they know well, but the main reason we have more accidents near where we live is much simpler: We have more accidents close to home because we generally spend more time driving close to home.

CHAPTER 8

Distributions

Distributions represent how a group of scores fall on a single variable. Although the term can have a number of meanings, it usually refers to ranking scores from smallest to largest while showing how many scores fall at specific points or within specific ranges. One of the most common methods for displaying a distribution of scores is a *histogram,* which is a method for visually reporting the number of scores (i.e., frequency) falling at specific points or within specific ranges.

Figure 8.1 is an example of a histogram that displays scores on an Ambition scale for over 30,000 managers around the world.

The table is from a statistical program called Statistical Package for the Social Sciences (SPSS) and presents results on the Ambition scale from the Hogan Personality Inventory. Scores represent how driven, competitive, and goal oriented a person is at work.

In this case, the graph reports Ambition scores as cumulative percentages that indicate where a person stands compared to scores from workers

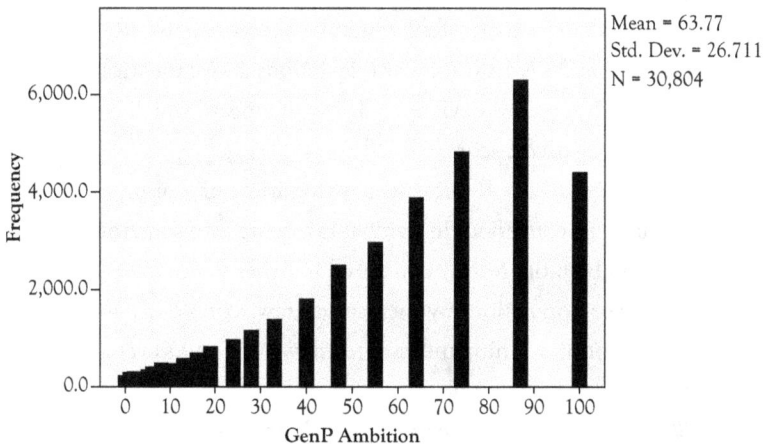

Figure 8.1 Ambition scores for managers

is all different jobs around the world. The most common percentile scores for managers is actually very high at 87 percent, while over 4,000 managers from the sample have scores of 100 percent (indicating that they received the highest score possible on the scale). Furthermore, very few managers are low on Ambition, with only a few hundred scores out of over 30,000 falling below the 10th percentile.

This confirms what many would probably assume, which is that managers, on average, tend to be much higher on Ambition compared to the general workforce. It also illustrates how one fairly simple graph can be used to quickly and easily summarize over 30,000 cases of data. And notice that the average score is only 63.77 percent, so while a majority of scores fall above that, there are still enough scores at the low end of the distribution to bring the overall average much closer to 50 percent.

Distributions serve as the basis for many statistical tests and are closely tied to two highly related topics: standardized scores and hypothesis testing. Key terms from each are presented as follows, although standardized scores and hypothesis tests are covered as separate parts in this chapter.

Key Terms

- *z-scores*: Represent how far away a score is from the mean in terms of standard deviations. For example, if the mean score on an assessment center is 25 and the standard deviation is 3, a raw score of 28 would be the equivalence of a z-score of 1.00 (and a raw score of 22 would be a z-score of −1.00). This means that 28 is 1.00 standard deviations above the mean and 22 is 1.00 standard deviations below the mean, which is why it has a negative z-score.
- *Standardized score*: Represents a wide variety of scoring methods used to convert an individual raw score into something that can be more readily compared to other scores from a sample or population. By themselves, raw scores don't always carry a lot of meaning unless one knows the scale's average and standard deviation.
- *Skew or skewness*: The degree to which one tail of a distribution is longer than the other. For example, household incomes

in the United States are often skewed, with most people falling around $35 to 75k and only a small percentage falling well above that range, but that small number can be well above it such as into the millions. So at $200k+, those small number of individuals are more than $100k above the mean, but it isn't possible to be below the mean by that far, so the distribution has a positive skew, meaning the distribution is tallest in the $37 to 75k region but has a small percentage of very high earners well above that. Ambition in the previous example had a negative skew because there is a small number of scores that are well below the average but a large percentage falling toward the upper end of the scale.

- *Kurtosis*: An indication of how tall or flat a distribution is. When most scales fall around the mean, the distribution appears tall and is called "leptokurtic." When scores are very spread out, the distribution appears more flat and called "platykurtic," like a plateau.

- *A normal distribution*: Also known as the Gaussian distribution, the normal distribution is a symmetrical distribution (meaning that the low end is a mirror image of the high end) where the mean, median, and mode all fall in the middle. If scores have been converted to z-scores, then that middle point has a z-score of 0.00 and the standard deviation is 1.00. This provides a nice way to put a variety of different scores onto the same metric so they can be compared, because being 1.00 standard deviations above the mean on one variable is similar to being 1.00 standard deviations above the mean on another variable regardless of the original range and distribution of the original raw scores.

- *The bell curve*: The bell curve is just another name for the normal distribution, although it should be noted that other distributions can also be bell shaped. Many naturally occurring variables tend to follow the bell curve (e.g., height and weight, blood pressure, most standardized test scores).

- *Statistical significance*: The probability, from 0 to 100 percent, that any observed differences between groups on a measure or association between multiple measures is simply due to chance caused by sampling error. In other words, if testing a diet pill, perhaps people who took the pill just happened to lose more weight that people who received a sugar pill, which would still have been the case if neither group participated in the experiment. A significance test tells us how likely it is that any differences we see between groups in terms of weight loss is real or simply due to chance. Each of the statistical tests covered in later chapters (9 to 13) result in significance tests.

- *Alpha*: The statistic most often tied to significance tests. Alphas range from 0.00 to 1.00. These scores represent the likelihood (i.e., percent chance) that an alternative hypothesis (see the following) is true. Typically, alphas of 0.05 or less are interpreted as "statistically significant." This means there is less than a 5 percent chance that any difference between groups or association between measures is simply due to chance, thereby allowing you to conclude that groups really are likely different or variables really are likely related to one another.

- *One-tailed versus two-tailed test*: One-tailed tests are tests that an effect occurs in a specific direction (e.g., Group 1 scores are higher than Group 2 or two variables are associated so that, as values on one increase, values on the other also increase). Two-tailed tests are tests that an effect is significant but could be in either direction (e.g., either group could be higher than the other or two measures are significantly associated with one another, but as one increases, the other could either increase or decrease).

- *Hypothesis*: A research question one tests through various statistical analyses (such as those in Chapters 9 through 13 of this book).

- *Null hypothesis*: A statement that nothing is occurring between variables, such as that groups are not different on an outcome or that two variables are not related to one another.

- *Alternative hypothesis*: A statement that there is a relationship between variables, such as that groups are different or that variables are related.

- *Type 1 error*: Rejecting a null hypothesis that is actually true. In other words, it is when a researcher finds a random difference or association that is purely due to chance, but large enough they conclude it must be real. So along those lines, if you are more strict in selecting what alpha you need to determine your results are significant (e.g., you decide ahead of time your alpha will be .01—reflecting only a 1.00 percent chance your results are due to random error), then the more likely it is that you will avoid committing a Type 1 error.

- *Type 2 error*: The failure to reject a null hypothesis that is false. In other words, the difference or association a researcher is testing might be real, but it either doesn't show up in their data due to chance or their sample size is too small, which means they find a difference but it's not large enough to conclude that it isn't simply due to sampling error.

Examples

Part 1: Standardized Scores

Tables 8.1 and 8.2 present examples of common standardized scores. With Sten scores, individuals receive a score of 1 to 10 on a variable based on their z-score on that variable. Stanine scores are very similar but are usually on a 1 to 9 scale and based on a specific distribution of relative frequencies, or percentages. For example, if a person's score on a variable is 0.60 standard deviations above the mean on a variable, their Sten score would be 7 (out of 10) and their Stanine score would be 6 (out of 9). A score that is 1.60 standard deviations below the mean would receive both a Sten and Stanine score of 2, and both be in or very near the bottom 10 percent of the distribution.

Standard scores often mean very little unless one knows the measure's mean and standard deviation, or as in the previous cases, the percentage of scores that fall within different ranges. For example, without knowing that average scores on the SAT, a common college entry exam used throughout the world, are approximately 500, there is no way of knowing if a score of 400 is above or below average. As it turns out, the SAT generally fits a pattern where the average scores is very near 500 and the standard deviation

Table 8.1 Sten scores

Sten	1	2	3	4	5	6	7	8	9	10
z-scores	<−2.0	−2 to −1.5	−1.5 to −1.0	−1.0 to −.5	−.5 to 0	0 to +.5	+.5 to +1.0	+1.0 to +1.5	+1.5 to +2.0	>+2.0
Percent	2.3	4.4	9.2	15.0	19.2	19.2	15.0	9.2	4.4	2.3

Table 8.2 Stanine scores

Stanine	1	2	3	4	5	6	7	8	9
Standard score	below −1.75	−1.75 to −1.25	−1.25 to −.75	−.75 to −.25	−.25 to +.25	+.25 to +.75	+.75 to +1.25	+1.25 to +1.75	above +1.75
Percent	4	7	12	17	20	17	12	7	4

is very near 100, so a 400 is actually equivalent to being about 1.00 standard deviations below the mean. But you need to know the mean and standard deviation to have any idea of what a score of 400 means.

Part 2: The Normal Distribution

Researchers also use distributions to represent how they expect scores on a variable to fall under certain circumstances. The most common example of such a distribution is the normal distribution, which itself has a number of very unique and specific properties. Figure 8.2 presents the picture that most people are familiar with regarding the normal distribution.

The normal distribution represents data that tend to center around one central value. There are the same number of cases above and below the mean, and fewer cases as a score gets further and further from the mean. This is why the mean, median, and mode are all the same value. There is also a specific percentage of scores in between any two z-scores. For example, 34.1 percent of all scores fall between a positive z-score of −1.00 and the mean (which again, is a z-score of 0.00). Because it is symmetrical, 34.1 percent of all scores also fall between a positive z-score of 1.00 and the mean. If you add those two up, you can see that 68.2 percent of all scores fall within one standard deviation of the mean for any measure that follows the normal distribution.

The percentage of scores falling within the tails is also very important. For example, 2.5 percent of all scores fall above a z-score of 1.96.

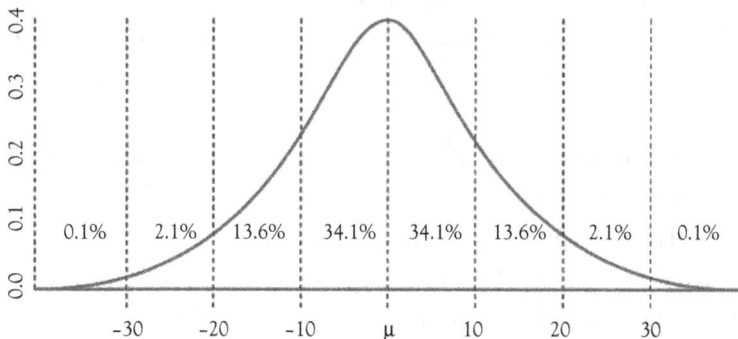

Figure 8.2 The normal distribution or bell curve

So likewise, 2.5 percent fall below a negative z-score of 1.96, meaning that 5.00 percent of all score fall either below -1.96 or above 1.96. Some statistical tests, such as t-tests (Chapter 9), use values like this to help determine if we can conclude that groups are likely statistically different from one another. This leads us to the importance of distributions for hypothesis testing.

Part 3: Hypothesis Testing

When conducting an analysis, we typically have a null hypothesis but can have more than one alternative hypothesis. For example, consider a test of whether or not computerized instruction leads to greater learning compared to traditional classroom-based instruction. Our outcome or criterion measure is scores on a post-training examination. To examine this question, a researcher randomly assigns two-class sections to receive classroom-based instruction and two classes to receive training via a new computerized course.

> Null hypothesis (often designated as H_0): Scores on the post-training examination will be the same regardless of instructional method.
>
> Alternative hypothesis #1 (often designated as H_1): Scores on the post-training examination will be higher for those who received computerized instruction compared to those who received traditional classroom-based instruction.
>
> Alternative hypothesis #2 (or H_2): Scores on the post-training examination will be higher for those who received traditional classroom-based instruction compared to those who received computerized instruction.

One could produce a longer more complex list of hypotheses by adding a third group, such as asking another two classes to simply learn their material by reading a text book, but that would also require more subjects to fill out more groups. So the best approach is often to just focus on the specific question at hand and try to control for anything else that could otherwise affect the study's results.

Furthermore, when examining differences between these two groups, it would be rare that both just happen to produce the exact same average post-training scores. Statistical analyses help determine the probability, or likelihood, that any differences a researcher finds are due to chance rather than true differences between conditions (e.g., that computerized instruction really did work better).

This is where distributions come into play. With a large enough sample, the distribution you use to test for statistical significance between two groups, which is a t-distribution (see Chapter 9), actually looks like the normal distribution. The product of a t-test is a t-score. The larger your difference between groups, the larger your t-score will be. With big enough samples, you can actually use the normal distribution to determine if your t-score is large enough that you can conclude your group differences are not likely due to chance—which means you would reject your null hypothesis and conclude that there is likely a difference between your groups.

In other words, if you have a large enough sample, you can conclude that your group differences are statistically significant if your t-score is either less than a negative—1.96 or greater than a positive 1.96. With smaller samples, this threshold can be higher. But the main point is that t-score helps you determine the likelihood that the groups differences you find are due to chance. If that t-score is large enough, which can be either positive or negative, then it falls within those most extreme ranges on the normal distribution. And if it is within the most extreme 5 percent (either the bottom 2.5 percent on the low end or the top 2.5 percent on the high end), then we generally conclude that our group differences are not due to chance but because one instructional method actually works better than the other.

Researches can also decide to set more extreme ranges, such as using an alpha of 1.00 percent. In this case, your t-score would need to be even higher—around 2.58—to reject your null hypothesis and conclude that group differences are not likely due to chance. Furthermore, different analyses generally work the same way but often based on different distributions that have different shapes and where different points represent the likelihood that results are simply due to chance.

For example, we use a similar approach when looking at potential associations between multiple measures. If one examines the relationship between time spent studying and post-training examination scores, the null hypothesis would be that time spent studying and examination scores are not related. The alternative hypothesis would likely be that, as time spent studying increases, examination scores also tend to increase. Again, you are likely to find some small association between any two measures, but you can use an r-score from a correlation (see Chapter 13) to determine if this association is simply chance or likely represents an actual relationship between the variables. In other words, can studying really help someone on this post-training test?

Be on the Lookout

Part 1: Climate Change

Climate change continues to be a hot topic in a variety of fields under behavioral sciences, such as environmental studies, political science, psychology, and sociology. Both proponents and detractors of climate change regularly throw out numbers to support their claims. For example, recent statistics indicate that 2015 was the hottest year in U.S. history. Yet, there are thousands of examples of different U.S. cities hitting new record lows for specific dates throughout the year. How is it possible?

Part 2: Extrasensory Perception

In 2011, Daryl Bern at Cornell published a study in the Journal of Personality and Social Psychology that presented what appears to be evidence for extrasensory perception, or in this case, the ability to see into the future. The study examined something familiar to all of us, which is that we remember words better when we rehearse their meanings. Of course, this typically means we rehearse the words before we are tested. In his study, however, Dr. Bern found that subjects tested better on word meanings even if they rehearsed them *after* they were tested, as opposed to no rehearsal after testing.

But to perhaps few people's surprise, several attempts to replicate these findings resulted in a failure to reject the null hypothesis (i.e., no significant effects of post-testing rehearsal). In other words, after trying to replicate the same process and procedures, a handful of researchers failed to find similar results. Of perhaps bigger concern, however, is that at least some have claimed that attempts to publish their nonsignificant findings met with failure, even in the same journal. Why might that be the case and what are the bigger implications concerning results we see on a daily basis, even in academic outlets?

Answers

Part 1: This is simply a matter of outliers. By definition, outliers do not occur that often, but they do occur, even if just by chance. So, if you were to look at all low temperatures for all 20,000 plus cities in the United States for every day of the year, there will inevitably be thousands of examples, out of the hundreds of thousands you could look at, that would have reached new record lows on that one specific day at that one specific location. Granted, given that it was the hottest year on record, there would be several times more record highs. But the fact is, outliers would still occur on both sides.

Part 2: There is no surprise here that one might find significant results even if the effect they are testing either doesn't exist or is small in magnitude. In other words, this is likely an example of a Type 1 error where, due to sampling error, the groups who studied the words afterward the test simply did better initially on the test compared to those who didn't study afterwards. In other words, there simply happened to be more people who know the words in those poststudy groups due to random chance, even despite the best of controls and large sample sizes used in the study. This is a good example, therefore, of how we can never scientifically prove anything because all statistics are based on probability and even the rarest of occurrences will sometimes still happen.

But with this example, it is also worth noting that nonsignificant results often have a more difficult time getting published in academic journals that require other professors and researchers to review the work (often call "peer-review journals"). So, if by random chance, a researcher finds significant results and publishes them, it is much harder for those who cannot replicate the results of the previous study to publish their own findings. In fact, at least one researcher claimed to have been rejected for publication because, at least in part, Dr. Bern was one of the peer-reviewers for their piece. True or not, many experts in a given field often serve as reviewers for topics in that same field, which can make it even more difficult to publish studies with results that contradict previous research. Of even bigger concern, however, are all of the results we are flooded with each day that no one, especially the person presenting them, has ever tried to replicate.

CHAPTER 9

T-Tests

One of the simplest and most common statistical analyses is a *t*-test, which helps determine if two groups are different on a continuous outcome. Examples are differences in test scores between two different classes, changes in blood pressure based on one group receiving a medication and other group receiving a sugar pill, or changes in anxiety levels before and after relaxation training.

There are three main types of *t*-tests. A *one-sample t-test* compare's one group's mean score to a known population score. It's the simplest form of *t*-test, but also probably the rarest. But it is useful on occasion when you have a lot of pre-existing data and want to see how well a new group might fit within this larger population. For example, one might use a one-sample *t*-test to determine if examination scores for one class differ significantly from several previous sections of the same course after some kind of treatment (i.e., does the average score from a new online section of a class differ from previous scores from several dozen regular sections?).

More commonly, *t*-tests are used to compare means between two specific groups. This is called an *independent samples t-test*. These are commonly used for experiments to compare a group receiving some kind of treatment, such (a) if a group of employees receiving computer training do better on a test of Excel skills than a group who does not receive training, (b) if individuals who receive a new drug have lower cholesterol than individuals who receive a sugar pill, or (c) if consumers who try a new toothbrush think their teeth feel cleaner than people who continue to use the old toothbrush. As outlined in Chapter 8, we would never expect two large groups to have the exact same average scores because of sampling error. So when we do find a difference, an independent *t*-test tells us how likely it is that this difference is simply due to random error, or chance.

The final kind is a repeated measure *or paired samples t-test.* Paired samples *t*-tests are similar to independent samples *t*-tests in that we test average differences on two variables, but in this case, both variables typically come from the same sample, usually in form of data collected from people at two different points in time (e.g., before and after training or before and after receiving some kind of treatment). For paired samples *t*-tests, we calculate the difference between scores at Time 1 and Time 2 for each person, such as to what degree their Excel skills change after Excel training or to what degree their cholesterol decreases after taking a new cholesterol medicine. Again, we wouldn't expect everyone's scores to be the exact same both times, but a paired samples *t*-test tells us the likelihood that any change we do see is simply due to chance.

Like many other statistical techniques, *t*-tests produce an alpha we can use to determine how likely it is that any difference between groups is simply due to chance. This alpha is impacted by what we call the effect size, which is the size of the differences between groups in this case, and by sample sizes. Larger effects and larger sample sizes result in lower alphas, meaning it is less likely that a difference is simply due to chance. With *t*-tests, the magnitude of the effect is determined by the standard difference in group means. So, it is not just the difference in average scores between the two groups that matter, but how that difference compares to the overall variance (see Chapter 7) in scores for all subjects in both groups. The more spread out the scores are, the lower the magnitude of the difference and the less likely that results will be statistically significant.

Key Terms

- *Effect size*: The magnitude of the difference between groups on a measure or the magnitude of the association between multiple measures.
- *d-scores (or difference scores)*: A standardized difference score (i.e., the raw score difference divided by the standard deviation of a measure). In terms of *t*-tests, *d*-scores represent our effect size and tell us the difference between our means in terms of how many standard deviations the two group averages are apart.

Examples

Consider examination scores from two sections of the same Introduction to Psychology course taught by two different instructors: Dr. Smith and Dr. Johnson (see Table 9.1). We can use a *t*-test to determine how likely the difference between scores is simply due to chance.

The *t*-test results for this example are significant ($p < 0.01$). Because our alpha (p) is less than 0.01, there is less than 1 percent chance that the observed difference in scores between the two sections is due to chance. In other words, Dr. Smith's class scored significantly higher than Dr. Johnson's class to a degree that we call statistically significant.

When interpreting results from a *t*-test, one must be very careful to consider why any differences between groups might exist. For example, consider the previous results. At face value, it would seem as though Dr. Smith is a more effective instructor because examination scores from his class are significantly higher than scores from Dr. Johnson's class. But, what if there is something unique about Dr. Smith's class? Perhaps he focuses more on teaching to the examination, or his class is an honor's class where Dr. Johnson's is not. As with any statistical analysis, we must try to account for unforeseen variables, like teaching to the examination or something unique about one of our groups, which account for the observed effect.

Be on the Lookout

Table 9.2 shows average scores on the SAT, a common college entry exam in the United States, from 1998. These results pertain to findings that, throughout the 1990s, average state spending per student was negatively correlated with SAT performance. As seen in the figure, average scores for

Table 9.1 Average examination scores from two different sections of the same course

Section #	Instructor	Class size	Mean score	Standard deviation score
1	Dr. Smith	22	94.32	10.04
2	Dr. Johnson	21	80.90	12.36

Table 9.2 Average SAT scores from New Jersey and North Dakota in 1998

State	Rank in spending	Average verbal	Average math
North Dakota	45th	590	599
New Jersey	2nd	497	508

Table 9.3 Average SAT participation rates

State	Participation rate (%)	Average verbal	Average math
North Dakota	5	590	599
New Jersey	79	497	508

North Dakota and New Jersey do seem to indicate that higher spending per student might actually result in lower SAT scores. Other than a direct causal relationship (i.e., North Dakota students did better because their state spent less per student), what else might account for this statistically significant difference?

Answer

Colleges in many states do not require the SAT. Whereas the SAT is more popular on the coasts, states in center of the nation traditionally rely more on another common college entry exam, the ACT. North Dakota, as shown in Table 9.3, favored the ACT throughout the 1990s. So, only students in North Dakota who were likely to apply to universities that are far away were likely to take the SAT. As it turns out, many of those students do so because they are the best and brightest and, therefore, are more attracted to prestigious universities with higher admission standards. Because many of these universities are on the east or west coast, they are also more likely to require the SAT. In other words, high school students from North Dakota were more likely to score well on the SAT in 1998 because they were more likely to represent the small percentage of students from the state who were considering applying to more prestigious schools.

CHAPTER 10

Analysis of Variance

Analysis of variance (ANOVA) is similar to a *t*-test, but can be used to compare more than just two groups. It can also be used to examine multiple predictors at once. And similar to *t*-tests, there are three different kinds of ANOVAs.

A *one-way ANOVA* compares multiple groups represented by only one independent variable, such as multiple instructors of the same course.

A *multivariate ANOVA* compares multiple groups represented by two or more independent variables, such as both instructor and morning versus afternoon sections (see the following). Multivariate ANOVAs also allow us to test for interactions between multiple variables. This means that the relationships between scores on one independent variable and an outcome depend on scores on another independent variable. For example, anxiety medicine can often do wonders for people who have high levels of anxiety to start with. The means there is a negative correlation between anxiety and medicine where the more medicine a person takes, the lower their anxiety. But, there is almost no relationship for people who are naturally more calm and relaxed. For these individuals, there is almost no correlation between the anxiety medication and actual anxiety. This means there is an interaction between a person's natural anxiety level and the effect of anxiety medications.

Finally, much like a repeated-measures *t*-test, a *repeated-measures ANOVA* tests the same individuals multiple times. Rather than just giving people anxiety medicine and testing their stress levels at one point down the road, it would be more ideal to repeatedly test their stress levels before they start the medicine, as soon as they start taking it, and then regularly throughout the duration of their treatment. This allows you not to just examine the overall change in anxiety at the end of treatment, but test for different patterns of responses from different people throughout the course of their treatment.

ANOVA also allows us to include covariates, or control variables, in our analyses. *Covariates* are variables that are associated with an outcome of interest but whose influence a researcher wants to remove from analyses. This allows you to more clearly see the relationship between other variables of interest. For example, there are a number of variables that can influence a person's income, such as industry, age, and even things like their parents socioeconomic status. If a researcher wanted to determine the impact of education level on annual income, he or she might first want to control for all of these other variables, meaning to statistically remove any influence they have on the outcome variable. In other words, when treating industry, age, and socioeconomic status as control variables, analyses can statistically remove their effect on income. Then what is left is a more straightforward examination of the true relationship between just education and income, after controlling for the effects of these other variables.

Also, when repeatedly testing a person's stress levels to determine the impact of anxiety levels, one might use results from the first round of testing, before they start taking the medicine, as a covariate to establish everyone's initial base rate. Then subsequent results more clearly indicate overall changes in stress level regardless of each subject's starting point.

ANOVAs produce one or more *F*-scores and an accompanying alpha for each independent variable and each interaction. *F*-scores are similar to *t*-scores (see Chapter 9) but account for overall differences across all levels of an independent variable or the overall impact of potential interactions between independent variables, see the following example.

Key Terms

- *Main effect:* The effect, or difference in scores, associated with each independent variable.
- *Interaction:* When the impact of one independent variable on an outcome of interest is dependent on another independent variable; again, see the following example.
- *Interaction effect:* The effect, or impact on scores, of an interaction.
- *Post hoc tests:* A set of procedures for determining if, when there is a significant main effect on a variable with more than two possible scores, there are differences between each

potential pairing of scores. For example, one could try two different dosage levels of an anxiety medicine as well as including a control group in an experiment. If there is a main effect for the medicine, that difference could be for a number of reasons, such as simply taking the medicine helps, or taking only the higher dosage helps, or taking the moderate dosage helps; but, the higher dosage helps more. In other words, one group might be different from the other two or all three groups could be different from one another. The problem with just running *t*-tests to examine all possible differences between groups is that you would then have to run three different *t*-tests (e.g., control group compared to the low dosage group, control group compared to the high dosage group, and the low dosage group compared to the high dosage group), essentially multiplying your chance of Type 1 error by three. If you have four groups, you will have six different potential comparisons, thereby roughly multiplying your changes of Type 1 error by six. Post hoc tests help control the inflated Type 1 error by adjusting alphas for each comparison based on a different formals. There are several different kinds of post hoc tests someone can run, but the most common are least significant difference (LSD), Bonferroni, and Tukey.

- *ANCOVA:* Analysis of covariance (ANCOVA) is similar to ANOVA but includes covariates; so, one can identify the effects of an independent variable on an outcome of interest after the effects of these covariates have been statistically removed.

- *MANOVA:* Multivariate analysis of variance (MANOVA) is like ANOVA but with multiple outcome measures. For example, a researcher might want to determine the impact of education and parents' socioeconomic status on later career success but define success with multiple variables such as income, prestige, and job level. A significant MANOVA would indicate that, in general, both predictors impact career success, at which point the researcher would basically have to break his or her outcome variables up again and run separate

ANOVAs to determine which predictors actually impact which outcomes and to what degree.

- *MANCOVA:* Multivariate analysis of covariance (MANCOVA) is like MANOVA but with the inclusion of covariates.

Examples

To expand on the example provided in the previous section, consider average examination scores from six different sections of an Introduction to Psychology class. There are now three different instructors. Each one has one morning class and one evening class. Table 10.1 presents class sizes, class means, and standard deviations.

In this case, the main effect for instructor is significant ($p < 0.01$) but the main effect for time of day is not ($p = 0.73$). This indicates that the instructor does have a significant impact on course performance but time of day does not. Post hoc tests also indicate there is not a significant difference in average examination scores for classes taught by Dr. Smith and Dr. Jones, but average examination scores for both instructors are significantly higher than average scores for classes taught by Dr. Johnson.

With this example, there is also a significant interaction effect ($p < 0.01$). Interactions between two variables are usually easiest to see by graphing mean scores. Figure 10.1 shows, Dr. Smith's morning class scored significantly higher than his afternoon class, but Dr. Jones' afternoon class

Table 10.1 Examination scores from six different sections of the same course

Section #	Instructor	Time period	Class size	Mean score	Standard deviation score
1	Dr. Smith	Morning	22	94.32	10.04
2	Dr. Johnson	Morning	21	80.90	12.36
3	Dr. Jones	Morning	19	82.42	16.21
4	Dr. Smith	Afternoon	19	82.32	11.39
5	Dr. Johnson	Afternoon	20	77.95	23.07
6	Dr. Jones	Afternoon	23	92.82	7.83

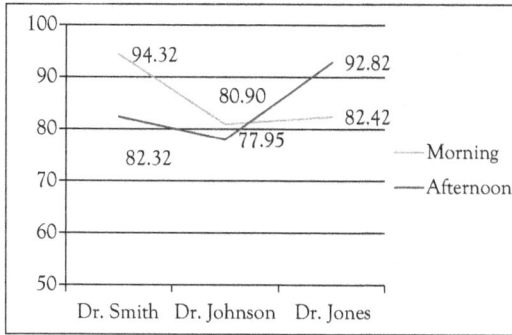

Figure 10.1 Average examination scores plotted on a line graph

scored significantly higher than her morning class. So, although we see no significant difference between scores for these two instructors when averaged across both of their sections, there is clearly a difference when time of day is taken into account.

Unequal sample sizes can cause problems with ANOVAs, but there are statistical corrections that most statistical programs run automatically. And as with other statistical analyses, one must always be aware of any unforeseen confounding variables that account for differences between groups. For example, not taking time of day into account would have potentially led to misleading results in the previous example. If only looking at morning classes, one would have likely concluded that Dr. Smith was the most effective instructor. But if collecting data only from afternoon classes, Dr. Jones clearly looks the best. And if sampling both classes but not including time of day as a variable, we would likely conclude that Dr. Smith and Dr. Jones are both more effective than Dr. Johnson, but would miss the very important distinction that this is highly dependent on time of day, because neither are more effective that Dr. Johnson at different times. And furthermore, perhaps Dr. Johnson does particularly well in other situations, such as evening or online classes. We would need more data representing more scenarios to test this research question.

Be on the Lookout

Consider an example where a researcher wants to study how various components of meeting someone for the first time influences that person's

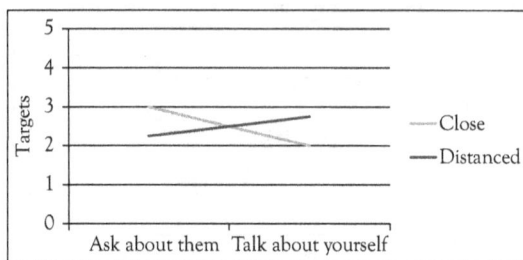

Figure 10.2 Average impression ratings plotted on a line graph

impression of who they are meeting. The researcher uses a simple *2 × 2 design*, meaning there are two independent variables comprised of two groups each. In this case, those groups are (1) physical proximity—close versus distanced and (2) topic of conversation—ask about the other person versus talking about him or her. Overall impression is measured using a 0 (very poor) to 5 (exceptional) rating scale. Results are presented in Figure 10.2.

This is an example of a "crossover" or "disordinal" interaction, meaning that when graphing group averages across the four possible scenarios, the lines cross. Such an interaction represents a pattern of results where the relationship between one independent variable and an outcome of interest clearly depends on the other independent variable. In this case, if another researcher were to repeat the previous study but only look at one independent variable at a time, how would that impact his or her results?

Answer

As this example shows, failing to include important variables can dramatically influence the results a researcher gets and, consequently, how they interpret those results. For example, in this case, what would have happened if the individual conducting the study failed to take the initial message into account? If the person initiating the conversation always approached a person by introducing themselves, the results would indicate that keeping one's distance was preferable to being too close. However, if the person initiating the conversation always approached a person by asking the other person's name, a researcher might reach the exact opposite conclusion—that being close was better than keeping one's distance. And if not coding for topic of conversation, but allowing those helping with the study to sometimes ask about themselves and the other person, then the researcher would likely not find any significant results at all.

CHAPTER 11

Chi-Square

The primary difference between a Chi-square and t-test or analysis of variance (ANOVA) is that with Chi-square, all variables are categorical. Therefore, our primary research questions pertain to whether the number of people in different groups fit some kind of expected pattern.

There are two primary kinds of Chi-square. The first one is called a *goodness of fit test*, which typically only deals with one variable and tests the assumption that scores on that variable fit a predetermined set of expectations. For example, if we roll a set of two dices 30 times, we would expect each possible outcome to come up around 10 times (with 60 total possible rolls). Granted, very rarely would every single outcome come up exactly 10 times. A goodness of fit test, therefore, tells us if whatever differences we see from this expected outcome are simply the result of chance. Or it could be that there is something wrong die, causing one or more numbers to come up much more frequently than others. If results for each possible role are close to 10, such as 8, 11, 9, 10, 12, and 10, our Chi-square will be nowhere close to statistically significant. But if our results are 7, 5, 6, 9, 8, and 25, there is only a very small chance our results are just due to chance—far less than 1 percent in this case. In other words, it is much more likely that there is something wrong with one or both of our dices in this case.

The second type of Chi-square is a *test for independence*, which examines whether or not membership in groups based on two or more variables is somehow related to one another. For example, consider a study where you examine differences between gender and who people vote for in an election. In general, males are slightly more likely to be Republican and women to be Democrats in the United States, but this isn't necessarily true for all states and doesn't necessarily work out for all candidates. So consider an election whether there is only one Republican and one Democrat on the ballot. Now we ask 100 men and 100 women who they voted for. If there is no association between gender and who they voted for, we would expect approximately 50 males vote for each candidate and 50 females vote for each candidate. Granted, we know we're not likely to get exactly those numbers because of sampling error, but a Chi-square test for independence would tell us if the differences we see from that expected outcome are simply due to chance or if it's likely that there is an association between gender and which candidate voters selected.

As with the techniques covered in previous sections of this guide, a Chi-square analysis produces an alpha score that indicates how likely any deviation in results, compared to expected results, is simply due to chance.

Key Terms

- *Expected frequencies*: How subjects are expected to be divided in groups according to some null hypothesis, such as an equal number of people across all groups for a goodness of fit test for proportional distributions of people on one variable regardless of scores on another variable.
- *Observed frequencies*: How subjects or occurrences actually do divide out across groups, which is the number of people within each actual group.

Examples

For an example of using Chi-square to compare results on a variable to a predetermined outcome, consider a scenario where a researcher wants to know which of the six flavors of potato chip they prefer. If they conduct blind test tests on 300 people, their null hypothesis would be that people generally do not prefer any one brand over the others. This would result in approximately 50 people selecting each of the six brands. Table 11.1 presents their results.

Table 11.1 Taste testing results

Brand	1	2	3	4	5	6
# selecting that brand	48	62	31	52	64	43

The resulting Chi-square indicates there is far less than a 1 percent chance that their results are simply due to chance. An examination of the data shows that consumers generally preferred brands #2 and #5 while preferring #3 the least.

Now consider an example where a researcher wants to compare applicant interview scores, designated as pass or fail, to performance on an assessment center, also designated as pass or fail (see Table 11.2). If the two are unrelated, one would expect the same pass or fail ratio on the assessment center for those passing the interview and those not passing the interview.

The resulting Chi-square is statistically significant, which indicates the two are likely related. In other words, those passing the interview are also more likely to pass the assessment center. We can see how much more likely by calculating (a) the percentage of people passing the assessment center who failed the interview and (b) the percentage passing the assessment center who passed the interview. For those failing the interview, 16 out of 45 passed the assessment center (36 percent). For those passing the interview, 34 out of 55 passed the assessment center (62 percent). In other words, people who pass the interview are almost twice as likely to also pass the assessment center compared to those who do not pass the interview.

Granted, given that interviews and assessment centers commonly produce continuous rather than categorical scores, one could also use a correlation (Chapter 12) to examine the association between these two variables. But, saying that two scores are correlated at a certain level (e.g., likely around 0.30 for the preceding example) is often not as clear and direct as using something like the 2 × 2 table presented earlier where we can easily see that those passing the interview are also nearly twice as likely to pass the assessment center.

Table 11.2 Assessment center results

	Failed assessment center	Passed assessment center	Percent passing assessment center (%)
Failed interview	29	16	36
Passed interview	21	34	62

Be on the Lookout

Part 1

Chi-square often is, but usually shouldn't be, used when there are low base rates for any one group on either variable. Low base rates are the result of very few people falling within any particular group. This not only causes problems for the calculation of the statistic itself, but can lead to very misleading results.

For example, serious accidents and injuries can happen in many jobs but are rare. Consider a study examining the impact of safety training on serious accidents and injuries, which only occur approximately 1 percent of the time for this particular position (see Table 11.3). What happens when results change for only one or two people in this sample?

Table 11.3 Accident rates

	No major accidents or injuries	Had a major accident or injury	Percent with a major accident or injury (%)
No training	208	5	2.35
Received training	386	1	0.26

Part 2

As with most analyses, Chi-square results can be misleading when potential influential or confounding variables are ignored. One notorious example comes from a review of Berkeley admissions by gender based on data collected in 1973. Perhaps as much as any place at any time, Berkley in the 1970s was very concerned about equal treatment based on gender and race or ethnicity. Data presented in Table 11.4, therefore, could be perceived as a surprise, especially given such large sample sizes. Based on these data, results indicate that males were admitted at a significantly higher pass rate than females.

But, when broken down by department (see Table 11.5), pass rates suddenly appear very different. In fact, the analysis shows a slight, but still statistically significant, bias toward females. How is this possible?

Table 11.4 Overall pass rats for men and women

Gender	Applicants admitted	Pass rate (%)
Men	8442	44
Women	4321	35

Table 11.5 Pass rates broken down by specific departments

Department	Males applied	Males admitted (%)	Females applied	Females admitted (%)
A	825	62	108	82
B	560	63	25	68
C	325	37	593	34
D	417	33	375	35
E	191	28	393	24
F	272	6	341	7

Answers

Part 1

With these results, there is a significant Chi-square (p = 0.02) and an examination of the percentage of those with accidents shows that individuals who did not receive training are over nine times more likely to have a serious accident or injury than those who did receive training. Granted, these are impressive results and certainly indicate the training likely had some impact, or at least more likely than what one would expect due to chance. But, what if the research finds that a handful of people received training but were originally categorized as "No Training?" If that were true for just one person who had an accident (so now four people with injuries didn't receive training and two people with injuries did receive training), the Chi-square would no longer be significant (p = 0.19). In this case, those without training would only be about three times more likely to have had an accident or injury than those who received training, and we could no longer conclude that the results are statistically significant. This would still indicate that training may have had some impact, but the results now look very different based on just one person in a sample of 600.

And if you change data for just 2 people out of 600 so that 3 people with injuries didn't receive training and 3 did, it would appear as though the training had little to no impact.

Part 2

In this case, department serves as a confounding variable because males are much more likely than females to apply to departments with larger sample sizes and higher pass rates, such as Departments A and B. Women, on the other hand, are more likely to apply for departments with lower pass rates, such as E and F. So across the board, more males were accepted because they are far more likely to apply to departments with higher pass rates.

But when we examine results broken down by department, we can see that women were actually accepted more often in four of the six departments and were very close to males in the other two. In fact, women were significantly more likely to get into Department A, but far fewer women applied to that department than men.

CHAPTER 12

Correlation

Correlation might be the most common statistical technique used in the behavioral sciences. Technically, correlation is a set of different techniques we use to determine the relationship between two variables, which are usually continuous, in terms of what or to what degree they are associated. *Association* refers to the degree to which scores on one variable tend to either increase or decrease as scores increase on another variable. Correlations also serve as the basis for many other techniques, or at least serves as a way to help interpret and understand results from other more complex techniques (e.g., regression—Chapter 13).

Correlations produce an r-score (r) that range from -1.00 for a perfect negative relationship—meaning that as values on one variable increase, values on the other decrease at exactly the same proportion, to 1.00, or a perfect positive relationship—meaning that as values on one variable increase, values on the other variable also increase the exactly the same proportion. A correlation of 0.00 indicates two variables are not associated with one another at all.

Consider shoe size and a person's IQ (which are not correlated). As we've seen with other techniques, if we collect data from 100 people on both of these variables, we will likely still find a very small negative or positive correlation due to random chance. In rare occasions, we could find a stronger correlation if we just happen to assess enough people with big feet and high IQs, or vice versa. Therefore, correlations give us an alpha, which represents the likelihood that our results are simply due to chance, which helps us determine how confident we can be that an association between our variables actually exists.

One common example of a correlation is height and weight. As people's height increases, their weight also tends to increase, although this relationship is not a perfect correlation (it is actually around $r = 0.70$).

This suggests that taller people tend to weigh more, but not universally. Although it is certainly possible for someone who is six feet tall to weigh less than someone who is five feet tall, on average, people who are taller weigh more.

And even small correlations are not necessarily unimportant. As with other types of statistics, the practical importance of any result depends on what we are examining. Typically, correlations around 0.10 are considered small, those around 0.30 are considered moderate, and those of 0.50 or higher are considered strong. However, even small correlations might have practical significance. If the correlation between cholesterol medicine and an actual drop in cholesterol levels over time is only 0.10, that may still indicate that the drug is effective enough for some people to potentially save lives. The trick is then to conduct more extensive research to better determine who the drug helps and who should devote their time and efforts to exploring other treatment options.

Squaring a correlation often makes the result easier to interpret because a squared correlation (*r-squared* or r^2) indicates *the percentage of variance accounted for* in one variable by another variable. To illustrate variance accounted for, consider height and weight again, where $r^2 = 0.49$ (e.g., 0.70×0.70). This indicates that approximately half of the fluctuation in people's weight is accounted for by their height while the remaining 51 percent is accounted for by other factors such as diet, exercise, genetics, and so on. Granted, this phrase is a little misleading because it seems to imply causation even though we know we cannot determine causation from correlation (see Chapter 4). So, even though a more appropriate definition of r^2 would be something like "percentage of variance shared between variables," "percentage of variance accounted for" is still the phrase most commonly used to describe r^2.

Also, there are several different types of correlation. For the most part, these depend on the type of variables we are examining (e.g., ordinal, interval, or ratio scales). Most statistical programs automatically use the appropriate type of calculation based on the measures under examination. So as long as we've entered our data correctly, we usually don't have to worry about the differences in the specific techniques.

Key Terms

- Common types of correlations:
  - o *Person product-moment*: Used to calculate a correlation between two quantitative (i.e., interval or ratio) scales.
  - o *Spearman's rho*: Used to calculate a correlation between two ordinal scales.
  - o *Point-biserial*: Used to calculate a correlation between one nominal and one quantitative scale.
  - o *Phi Coefficient*: Used to calculate a correlation between two nominal scales with only two levels.
- *Covariance*: Another indication of the degree to which two measures are associated with one another. Usually, a correlation coefficient is essentially just covariance that has been converted into a –1.00 to 1.00 score.
- *Line of best fit*: A line you can draw through a scatter plot (see the following) that is mathematically as close as possible to all of the points representing data from each study participant on both variables. The line of best fit is often useful in helping visually represent relationships between variables. And when we draw it on a scatter plot, we can also easily see how closely individual scores fall to this line.
- *Range restriction*: When a researcher does not have a full range of scores on one or more variables under examination. Range restriction usually reduces the size of a correlation if one only has data from subjects at one end or another on either variable. But it can increase a correlation if a researcher is missing data in the middle ranges of either one or both variables.

Examples

Correlations can often be seen and understood best through *scatter plots*, which are graphical representations of where scores for individual subjects fall on two measures under examination. Figure 12.1 shows some examples.

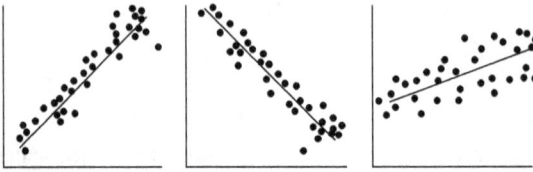

Figure 12.1 Examples of scatter plots representing different correlations

Figure 12.1 shows what a scatter plot would typically look like a strong correlation, including a line of best fit. From this, we can see that it is a positive correlation because the line goes up to the right and that most of the data points fall fairly close to the line. The closer points are to the line, on average, the stronger the correlation.

The second picture is similar but for a negative correlation because the line goes down as it goes to the right, indicating that as scores on the variable on the horizontal axis increase, scores on the other variable represented by the y-axis tend to decrease.

The third picture represents data for two variables that have a weak positive correlation. The line goes up to the right, but on average, points representing data for different subjects fall farther away from the line of best fit.

A fourth option would be data with missing points in the middle on both variables, which is a form of range restriction. An example would be having only scores in the bottom left and top right part of the first picture. However, the more common form or range restriction is missing data at either end of a variable. For example, the relationship between a person's body mass index (BMI) and their blood pressure is usually a strong positive correlation. But, if you measured both using only Olympic athletes, there would likely be little to no relationship because nearly everyone would have a very low BMI and a much lower than average blood pressure. For example, we know that the correlation between height and weight is around 0.70. But if you only collected data from preschoolers and NBA players, both in the same dataset, you would only have scores on the very low end of both variables and the very high end on both variables. The resulting correlation would likely be 0.90 or higher.

This shows why it's important to always interpret correlations with range restriction in mind.

Be on the Lookout

Part 1: Vaccinations and Autism

One topic that has received a lot of media attention over the last decade is the potential link between autism and vaccinations. As the number of children receiving vaccinations has steadily increased over the years, the number of children diagnosed with autism has also increased. There is no doubt, therefore, that the two are correlated. Yet, a number of published scientific studies find no direct link between the two, leading many prominent sources such as the Centers for Disease Control (CDC), the World Health Organization, the American Academy of Pediatrics, and even the Autism Science Foundation, to state there is currently no evidence that vaccinations are directly linked to autism. How is this possible?

Part 2: Churches and Bars

For a less serious example, consider the fact that, as the number of churches in a town increases, the number of bars usually increases as well. In other words, the two are also highly correlated. However, despite the many off-color explanations of this relationship we might be able to come up with, there is no clear reason to believe that going to church makes one more likely to go to bars, or the other way around. Yet, the correlation between the two is very real and consistent. How is this possible?

Answer

Both examples likely suffer from the same problem: there is a confounding variable that produces the correlation between the two variables under examination.

For the first one, better exposure to health care might increase both the number of vaccines administered each year and the number of children diagnosed with autism. That is one very likely reason why there could be a correlation between number of vaccinations per year and a wide range of different childhood diagnoses.

For the second example, the confounding variable is the size of the town. One would get the same result if replacing churches or bars with other common institutions such as gas stations, grocery stories, and so on.

CHAPTER 13

Regression

In its most basic form, regression is similar to correlation but usually involves associating multiple predictor variables with one criterion or outcome variable. Most regression techniques use a complex process involving matrix algebra that determines the best way to combine scores from predictors to produce a new score that correlates as high as possible with the outcome. If only using one predictor score, however, the result is the same as you would get with a correlation. But with more than one predictor, regression assigns weights that indicate how strongly each individual predictor is associated with the outcome score.

The resulting statistic (R) ranges from 0.00, which indicates there is no association between the outcome variable and any other predictor variable, to 1.00, which indicates the outcome variable can be perfectly predicted by one or more predictor variables. Like r-scores with correlation, one can square R to determine the percentage of variance in an outcome measure that is accounted for by a combination of all predictor measures.

Regression results can be illustrated using an equation, usually something similar to $\hat{y} = a + b_1 x$. In this equation, $\hat{y}$ is the predicted value of y, which represents the outcome variable of interest. So, y represents actual values on the outcome and $\hat{y}$ represents predicted values based on x, which is a person's score on a predictor variable. The other two components of the equation are a and b_1, where a represents an *intercept*, or $\hat{y}$ when x = 0, and b_1 represents the *slope* of x, or incremental increases in $\hat{y}$ with each one point increase in x. See the following example for a better illustration of this equation.

As mentioned, regression can include more than one predictor variable. The resulting equation is very similar but has additional components for each additional predictor variable (e.g., $\hat{y} = a + b_1 x + b_2 z$). In this case, z is the second predictor variable and b_2 represents its slope. In instances involving more than one predictor variable, the intercept (a) is the predicted value of y ($\hat{y}$) when both predictor variables (x and z) equal zero. For example, if you were trying to predict someone's annual income based on their education level and parent's socioeconomic status, your intercept would reflect you predicted value if both education level and parent's socioeconomic status is zero, which might not always be possible. But, your intercept still tells you what your predicted value would be if every other predictor variable actually could have a score of zero.

Also, like correlation, regression produces alphas to help determine if the association between variables is likely due to chance. When running a regression, you get an alpha for the overall model, which indicates whether or not the best possible combination of predictor scores is significantly related to the outcome variable. But you also get alphas for each predictor variable in the model, and can even examine interactions and covariates using increasingly complex regression models. This makes regression a very flexible analysis that can work with multiple variables and different types of relationships between those variables.

Key Terms

- *Simple regression*: Very similar to correlation in that there is only one predictor. So, like correlation, there are only two variables: one predictor and one outcome. One advantage of simple regression over correlation is that it can be used to create a regression line with both an intercept and slope. One can then use this line to graphically represent the relationship between the two variables, but also determine a specific predicted outcome score on the outcome variable for each point on the predictor variable (e.g., what is a person's predicted weight based on their height?).

- *Multiple regression*: Regression involving more than one predictor variable, but still only one outcome variable.

- *Beta weight*: A standardized slope or regression weight, meaning what the slope would be if all variables were first standardized or converted into z-scores (see Chapter 7). The advantage of beta weights is that they put all predictors on a common metric so that they can be more easily compared to one another to see which predictors account for the most variance in your outcome variable. In other words, they are a good way to see which predictor variables are actually most predictive of the outcome you care about.

- *Stepwise regression*: A set of different methods for identifying predictors to include in a regression model. Stepwise regression is useful when a researcher has a lot of potential predictor variables but wants to identify a small set that most effectively predict an outcome variable. It involves different procedures for including only variables that are most predictive and excluding those that no longer help predict the outcome variable once other predictors are already included in the model.

- *Dummy variables*: Categorical variables can be used as predictors in regression, but only when first converted into dummy variables. Dummy variables have only two potential values: 0 and 1. Each dummy variable represents membership into only one potential group on its associated categorical variable. For a categorical variable, regression requires a dummy variable for all but one group. So for example, if a researcher is examining the relationship between political affiliation and knowledge of U.S. history, he or she would first have to code people by political affiliation (e.g., Republican, Democrat, independent, or other). To include this variable in a regression equation, three dummy variables are required (e.g., one containing values of 1 for all Republicans and 0 for everyone else, one containing values of 1 for all Democrats and 0 for everyone else, and one containing values of 1 for all independents and everyone else). The resulting regression weights associated with each dummy variable help determine if being part of that specific group (e.g., republican, democrat, or independent) affects the outcome of interest. Results for the fourth group in this case, which would be "others," is reflected in regression results for people who have a zero on each of the other three dummy variables, which is why there is no need for a dummy variable for all four groups. In other words, that value is actually accounted for by the intercept.

- *Multiple regression*: This term can mean lots of different things. But typically, when people talk about multiple regression, they are talking about regression involving multiple variables entered into a regression equation through a series of steps. One of the most common uses of this approach is to determine if variables entered during later steps are associated with an outcome even after having already entered other predictor variables in earlier steps. This is often called incremental validity (see the following).

- *Change in R-square*: Regression produces not only alphas associated with each step but an alpha representing changes in prediction from one step to the next. This indicates whether new variables significantly predict an outcome variable even after other variables have been entered in previous steps.

- *Incremental validity*: For example, does an assessment center have incremental validity over the other three previous variables, meaning does it predict job performance "above and beyond" the other three variables, or after the effects of the other variables have already been taken into account? Consider a scenario where a researcher has success predicting job performance with scores on a cognitive ability test, a personality test, and an interview, but wants to see if prediction can be further increased by including scores from an assessment center. He or she would enter the first three predictor variables into the first step of a regression equation and then enter assessment center results into Step 2. A significant increase in prediction from Step 1 to Step 2 would indicate that assessment center results likely increases prediction above and beyond the original three predictors. But if there wasn't an increase in prediction, then there is likely no value to adding an expensive assessment center into a hiring process that already includes a cognitive ability test, a personality test, and an interview. This kind of regression analysis is also necessary for testing covariates, all of which have to be entered before entering predictor variables, and other relationships between variables such as interactions and curvilinear relationships (see the following).

- *Logistic regression*: A related but separate procedure for pre-dicting a categorical outcome variable. Logistic regression provides information concerning how likely individual subjects are to fit into specific groups. For example, you could gather data on several health related variables and then track them to see who has what ailments in the future. With this information, you could look at similar health-related information for new patients and predict their likelihood of having the same ailments down the road.

- *Curvilinear relationships*: Correlation and most simple regression analyses examine linear relationships between variables, or relationships that can be represented by a straight line (think of as height and weight). However, some relationships might be nonlinear, such as the relationship between tenure and the performance of athletes. For the most part, athletes tend to get better as they get more experience, but if they stay healthy long enough, their performance will eventually start to decrease as they age. In other words, there is a curvilinear relationship between age and performance in that performance increases with age up to a point, but then starts to decline. It is possible to test for such relationships using regression. To do so, one first squares the predictor variable of interest (e.g., age). The next step is to enter the original predictor into a regression equation as Step 1 and then its squared value as Step 2. If there is a significant increase in prediction with the squared term, then there is evidence of a curvilinear relationship. The resulting regression line can then be used to plot this relationship for easier interpretation.

Examples

To illustrate how a regression equation ($\hat{y} = a + b_1x$) works, consider an example where a researcher uses years of experience to predict job perfor-mance. One might assume that job performance increases to some degree with experience, but it is certainly not a perfect relationship because job performance is also impacted by a number of additional factors. In this case, *y* is job performance (measured on a 0 to 100 scale with an average score of 50) and x is years of experience (which ranges from 0 to 40 years). Based on data from 100 people, the resulting regression equation is $\hat{y}$ = 40 + 0.5x. The best predicted value for individuals with zero years of experience (x = 0) is designated by the intercept, which equals 40. So, people with no job experience tend to, on average, receive job performance ratings of 40 out of 100. Next, the slope (b_1) equals 0.5. This indicates that average job performance tends to increase 0.5 points for every one year of experience. So, if one wants to predict job performance for someone who has been on the job for 24 years (i.e., determine $\hat{y}$ when x equals 24), the result would be $\hat{y}$ = 40 + 0.5 * 24 = 52.

One could then expand on this equation by adding another variable: cognitive ability. Assume that cognitive ability also predicts job performance, and that ratings (represented by z, based on a test with a 0 to 100 score) are available for all 100 people in the sample. The resulting multiple regression equation is now $\hat{y}$ = 20 + 0.3x + 0.45z. Notice that when including cognitive ability, both the intercept and the slope for experience changes. This is usually because there is also a correlation between both predictors. For example, given that people with higher cognitive ability tend to do better, they may also be able to stay in the job longer. So, after including cognitive ability in the equation, experience is still predictive, but not as strongly. But, because there are now multiple predictor variables that are related to the outcome variable, prediction increases. So, to predict job performance for someone who has been on the job for 10 years and had a cognitive ability score of 85 out of 100, the result would be $\hat{y}$ = 20 + 0.3 * 10 + 0.45 * 85 = 61.25. This estimate should be more precise and accurate in terms of predicting this person's job performance because we are now accounting for multiple predictors.

One common concern with regression is known as *multicolinearity*, which essentially just means there can be problems when one or more predictor variables are strongly correlated with one another. In the previous example, the regression weight for experience changed when cognitive ability was added, but it didn't change dramatically and was still significant itself. However, if predictor variables are too highly correlated, then one predictor will not improve prediction much over the other. Instead, the regression weights for both will end up being unstable and could change dramatically with adding or taking out just one or two people from the sample.

And like correlation, regression only analyzes associations between variables. It does not imply causation. Although when speaking of regression, researchers often use terms like "predictor variables" and "outcome variables," that does not necessarily mean predictors actually cause changes in outcomes of interest.

Be on the Lookout

Some have claimed that one's job performance can be predicted through two unrelated types of intelligence: traditional IQ and emotional intelligence (EI or EQ). Because we know IQ generally accounts for about 15 percent of the variance in job performance ratings, some proponents of EQ have claimed that EQ must, therefore, account for the remaining 85 percent. What is wrong with this claim?

Answer

The problem is that IQ and EQ are not the only possible variables that influence job performance. Even if job performance could be measured perfectly, there are countless other variables that influence our work behaviors and, consequently, our performance on the job. Other common variables that influence work behaviors include experience, training, motivation, and the availability of necessary resources. So, while IQ might account for 15 percent of the variance in job performance, no one other variable accounts for the remaining 85 percent. Instead, a better approach would be to include both as predictors and see if EQ predicts performance above and beyond IQ—which it does to some degree, but usually only an additional 5 to 10 percent.

Final Notes on Presenting Your Own Results

This section covers a few remaining thoughts worth taking into consideration when reviewing data provided by others or presenting your own results.

- Garbage in garbage out (GIGO). Most people have heard of this term or phrase in other areas, and it's just as applicable in statistical analyses and results. Without good quality data to start with, results are meaningless. Even the slightest miscalculation or misalignment of data, such as failing to match up people's predictor scores with the correct outcomes, can throw off a study's results entirely.

- Don't take everything at face value. Hopefully, the examples presented throughout this book already make this point. But even when presented with results that don't seem extraordinary, it is worth always looking at things with a critical eye. Some key areas to consider are data quality, methods used to collect and analyze data, and the potential exclusion of things like confounding variables.

- When results don't look correct, they probably aren't. When you fully expect results to work out in a certain way and they don't, don't panic. The fact is, very unusual or odd looking results are the result of some sort of error the vast majority of the time. Granted, we sometimes find results we don't expect, which can be an exciting part of the research and discovery process. But, you should always double check your analyses and results. This is particularly true when your results seem odd or are unexpected. In other words, if a result looks wrong, more often than not, it is wrong.

- You probably don't need to be a statistical expert, but you might need access to one. Most people who work in behavioral sciences have at least some training on the techniques covered in this book, which also means anyone working in the area might be expected to demonstrate a basic understanding of the same concepts and techniques. But in most settings, not everyone is going to be expected to be a statistical expert. So, when you need help, ask for it.
- Get to know your data. One mistake many researchers make is to immediately begin running analyses (e.g., correlations, regressions, t-tests) as soon as they have a full dataset without first looking at their data. Before conducting an analysis on any variable, spend a little bit of time looking at the data for you variables. Look for potential outliers on either the lowest or highest end of a scale. Look for missing data. Look at the distribution of scores on each variable to see if anything else stands out as potentially wrong or problematic. When running correlations, look at a scatter plot to see if scores from one or two subjects clearly stand out from the rest. These basic reviews will not only help you become more familiar with your data, but are the best way to quickly identify potential mistakes.

There are a few critical considerations to keep in mind when presenting results to others:

- Know your audience: One of the biggest mistakes people make when presenting results is failing to take their audience into account. Before putting together a results presentation, identify your intended audience. Find out what their level of statistical sophistication is and prepare your materials accordingly. Perhaps even more importantly, find out ahead of time what they want to know. You might need to be prepared to present results in different ways to different audiences. For example, when writing results for a more academically inclined audience, clear details concerning your specific research questions, research strategy, sample, analyses, and results all matter. In contrast, when presenting results to a customer or group of coworkers, only the briefest descriptions are likely needed. In these cases, focus more on the meaning of the results and their impact for your audience members.

- Have a good summary: With any results presentation, a good abstract or executive summary is often the most important piece you will create. The fact is, your summary is all most people will read. As a result, it should briefly cover all major aspects of your study and analyses and their meaning to audience members.

- Don't skimp on interpretation: If you are presenting results to others, you are the expert. Especially early in their careers, many researchers tend to focus too much on the details of a study and leave it to their audience to draw their own conclusions. Don't be afraid to explain to your audience why you think your results are important to them.

- Use tables and figures when possible: If you can summarize results in a table or figure, do. Even journal article reviewers often recommend presenting results through tables and figures when possible. This not only helps put results into perspective, but is often easier on the reader. As a cautionary note, make sure that tables and figures are straight forward and easy to understand. Anyone with a basic understanding of a study should be able to look at a table or figure and quickly and easily understand the information presented.

- Keep things simple: It is often best to focus on one or two key points when presenting results. As with a good summary, a presentation should focus just on what is important to intended audience members and what those results mean to them.

- Aesthetics matter: The ability to conduct good research and present results in a visually appealing manner are two entirely separate and unrelated skills. As with running your own analyses, if you do not have a lot of experience with creating white papers or presentations, find someone who does and ask them for help.

- Don't be afraid to say you don't know the answer to a question: Especially when presenting results in front of others, most of us dread the possibility of being asked questions we don't know how to answer. But the best strategy is often the simplest, say that you don't know but will find out and get back to the person. Often the worst thing you can do in this situation is back yourself into a corner by saying something that doesn't end up making sense or simply isn't true. Furthermore, most people will appreciate it if you follow-up with them later because it shows you care about their question and that you care about them as an audience member. In other words, saying you don't know but will find out is often a good way of turning a potential negative situation into a positive one.

- Practice: The best way to make sure you are ready to present results to others is to have at least one or two people who represent your intended audience and review your results first. If you are submitting something for publication, ask some experienced researchers to review your manuscript before submitting it to a journal. If you are presenting results to a client, practice first using someone who will provide honest and constructive feedback. When conducting research, most of us are too close to the study to anticipate what questions others might have or what others might find confusing. The best way to prepare for these questions and avoid problems concerning potentially confusing results is to have others review your materials first.

Index

OTHER TITLES IN THIS CHILD CLINICAL PSYCHOLOGY "NUTS AND BOLTS" COLLECTION

Samuel T. Gontkovsky, *Editor*

Learning Disabilities
By Charles J. Golden, Lisa K. Lashley, Jared S. Link,
Matthew Zusman, Maya Pinjala, Christopher Tirado,
and Amber Deckard

Intellectual Disabilities
By Charles J. Golden, Lisa K. Lashley, Andrew Grego,
Johanna Messerly, Ronald Okolichany,
and Rachel Zachar

Momentum Press is one of the leading book publishers in the field of engineering, mathematics, health, and applied sciences. Momentum Press offers over 30 collections, including Aerospace, Biomedical, Civil, Environmental, Nanomaterials, Geotechnical, and many others.

Momentum Press is actively seeking collection editors as well as authors. For more information about becoming an MP author or collection editor, please visit http://www.momentumpress.net/contact

---

Announcing Digital Content Crafted by Librarians

Momentum Press offers digital content as authoritative treatments of advanced engineering topics by leaders in their field. Hosted on ebrary, MP provides practitioners, researchers, faculty, and students in engineering, science, and industry with innovative electronic content in sensors and controls engineering, advanced energy engineering, manufacturing, and materials science.

Momentum Press offers library-friendly terms:

- perpetual access for a one-time fee
- no subscriptions or access fees required
- unlimited concurrent usage permitted
- downloadable PDFs provided
- free MARC records included
- free trials

The **Momentum Press** digital library is very affordable, with no obligation to buy in future years.

For more information, please visit **www.momentumpress.net/library** or to set up a trial in the US, please contact **mpsales@globalepress.com.**